Professors
Can
Preach

Copyright © 1988 by Joe E. Trull

Published by Insight Press, Incorporated
P. O. Box 8369, New Orleans LA. 70182

Cover photograph by Breena Kent Payne

ISBN 0-914520-26-1

Library of Congress Cataloging-in-Publication
Number 88-081871

Printed in the United States of America

To The Faculty
of
New Orleans Baptist Theological Seminary
"by his appointment . . . herald, apostle
and teacher. . . ." (II Timothy 2:11).

CONTENTS

Preface

Why publish a book of sermons by seminary professors? The main reason is simple. They deserve to be read.

Twenty-five years of my ministry focused on writing, evaluating and delivering sermons. Like most pastors, I know a good sermon when I hear one. Three years of chapel services at New Orleans Baptist Theological Seminary have convinced me of one thing. Professors can preach!

Other reasons motivated this publication. The sermons provide strong models for students studying homiletics. Alumni will enjoy reading sermons of former professors. Pastors and preachers will find motivation for better preaching. Finally, if there exists anywhere a question about the quality of discipleship in the lives of our present seminary teachers, these messages should help answer that concern.

Each sermon was delivered in seminary chapel from 1985–1988. They are recorded basically as delivered, so that each may be "heard" as well as read.

The most difficult task was selection within the space allowed. A deliberate attempt was made to include a variety of sermon subjects, styles and biblical themes within five categories: evangelism and missions, doctrine, ethics and discipleship, pastoral and devotional. Diversity was also sought in faculty representation. Many excellent sermons could not be included because of these restrictions.

Several persons deserve gratitude for their assistance. Preaching professors Harold Bryson and Jerry Oswalt gave valuable advice and encouragement. Fisher Humphreys assisted often with publication procedures. Cheryl Dingus provided secretarial skills for compiling the finished product.

It is my hope and prayer God will bless you who read these sermons as much as the seminary family was "first-blessed" in hearing them.

Joe E. Trull
June, 1988

Introduction

The sermons found in this volume have all been preached in the chapel of the New Orleans Baptist Theological Seminary. These chapel services are held three days of every week, out of the four days on which classes meet. These services are intended to provide a break from the strictly academic approach of the classroom and are designed to give spiritual uplift and encouragement to students and faculty.

The professors who teach at New Orleans Baptist theological Seminary are persons who have lengthy local church experience in addition to terminal degrees in their chosen fields. A study done several years ago indicated that our professors average twenty-five years of service in the local church, twelve years each prior to becoming faculty members and the remainder in interims and other assigned responsibilities since coming to the campus. We believe that this forms an ideal background for the teaching and training of God-called men and women for service in the local church and the denomination.

These sermons are on a variety of subjects and each is from a different professor. They can be looked upon from the homiletical point of view, but the basic intention of each message was to provide encouragement and comfort, admonition and direction for those in attendance at chapel. It is highly possible that notes were taken or tapes ordered of many of these messages and they were refined for use in the churches served by the students!

Dr. Joe Trull, a long-time pastor and denominational leader who now teaches ethics on our faculty, has rendered a service in bringing this material together. I recommend the book to you from the standpoint of an intimate glimpse into the spiritual life and preaching ministry of each individual as well as an indication of the tang and zest of these services. The sermons were each delivered in the context of congregational singing, prayers, and musical numbers provided by soloists, ensembles, choirs, and handbells. These other elements of worship contributed greatly to the effectiveness of the messages on delivery.

Landrum P. Leavell II

The Mission Mandates of Our Lord

DR. A. J. GLAZE

This morning for our meditation, I would like to refer to three major mission mandates of our Lord. The first is found in the fourth chapter of John. After Jesus' initial encounter with the Samaritan woman, she left to call the townspeople to come and to see the one that had told her so much about herself. The disciples, who had gone to look for food, returned and offered him that which they had found. However, to their surprise, he was not hungry. They were perplexed, and he said to them:

> My meat is to do the will of him that sent me, and to finish his work. Say not ye, there are yet four months and then cometh the harvest. Behold, I say unto you lift up your eyes and look on the fields, for they are white already unto harvest (John 4:34).

The first mandate is to *LOOK* at the fields that are white unto harvest.

Matthew 9 records that Jesus went about the cities, taught in the synagogues, preached the gospel of the kingdom, and healed every kind of sickness and disease. Then he wrote:

> When he saw the multitude, he was moved with compassion on them because they fainted and were scattered abroad as sheep having no shepherd. Then said he unto his disciples, "The harvest truly is plenteous, but the laborers are few. Pray ye, therefore the Lord of

1

harvest that he will send forth laborers unto his harvest" (Matthew 9:36).

The second mandate is to *PRAY* that the Lord of harvest will send laborers into his harvest.

The third mission mandate is found in the last verses of Matthew. (It is also embedded in the longer conclusion to Mark.)

Go ye therefore and teach all nations, baptizing them in the name of the Father, and of the Son, and of the Holy Ghost (Matthew 28:19).

The Mark account puts it simply: "Go ye into all the world and preach the gospel to every creature" (Mark 16:15). The third mandate is to *GO*.

The key words for this morning are "Look," "Pray," and "Go." In the real sense, the imperative in Matthew's "Great Commission" is not found in the word "Go," which actually is a participle. Perhaps the meaning is found in "going," or "as you go" make disciples. Nevertheless, the three mandates stand as Christian imperatives: look, pray, and go (make disciples).

As I *look* back on an experience from Argentina, it almost seems as if it were a trip into yesterday. It was a long weekend holiday. We had packed the mission jeepster early. As soon as seminary classes were over that Wednesday, we left town, and by 3:30 p.m. had cleared the massive Buenos Aires traffic. We were five altogether: three missionaries, one national professor-pastor, and our host-guide, Sr. Glazner. Sr. Glazner, a Jewish businessman, philosopher, and pantheist, had invited us to accompany him to a little cabin he owned on the backside of nowhere, on a mountain trout stream in Central Argentina.

That night we took turns driving, for it was a long way to Mr. Glazner's place. The fact is, early the next morning we ran out of road, and it was still a two hour horseback ride to get to the cabin. All night Mr. Glazner sat in the front seat; he was the host and guide. As we took turns driving,

Mr. Glazner constantly bombarded us with questions about our beliefs. He was trying to understand our Christian faith through his philosophical background. During one of my turns, he looked at me and asked a question: "How can a good name like Glaze, be a Protestant Baptist and not a Jew?" That does pose a theological question. I have decided to consult my good colleague, Dr. Ed Glaze. Maybe he can help me find the answer!

During the night, as the hours and kilometers slipped by, the topic changed to the little community that was located at the end of the mountain road. It was a trading center for the mountain people, and Mr. Glazner suggested that we have a Christian service on Sunday when we returned from our camping expedition. It seemed good to us, and I think to the Holy Spirit, that we have an open air preaching service. Mr. Glazner said that there was an open area by the eating place of the community. He knew the mayor and could get the proper permission. He said that he could make a poster when we got there and that the news would spread throughout the area.

Early the next morning, as dawn arrived, we saw the mountains ahead. We ran out of paved road, graveled road, and finally even the winding mountain road. We came to a small community known as Yacanto. There it was: a few houses and the eating place. I'll call it a restaurant just in case a member of the Board of Trustees might be present (however, the sign in front said "Bar"). It was the local eating and drinking place. Across the street was a general store, and down the street was a small Catholic chapel that was padlocked. Not far from the chapel was a one-room school building. In front of the eating place were six horses tied to the hitching rail. There the road ended, and the mountaineers came in by horseback.

We walked in to the smell of coffee and freshly baked homemade bread. The owner of the little eating place smiled at Mr. Glazner and said, "I didn't think you would be here this early." But the table was set, and soon the coffee was poured. Mr. Glazner invited Juan, the owner of the horses (our next mode of transportation) to join us for an

Argentine breakfast. Filled with the conversation of the night, our Jewish friend looked at Juan and said, "Do you know Jesus Christ?" Juan scratched his head, and I remember his words distinctly: "I think so. Wasn't he through here several years ago?"

The expedition was over. It was Sunday. Juan had guided us, left us, and fortunately come back. I looked at the small mountain pony that I would be riding and really felt sorry for him. I felt that perhaps I should carry him instead of his carrying me! I don't think that little pony had ever carried a person as tall as I, and my six feet stance is not that large. Nevertheless, the saddle was small, and the stirrups could not be lengthened to match my legs. My knees were under my chin, and the toes of my boots would scarcely fit into the small opening of the stirrups. As we came back into town, this caravan of North American cowboys, I saw that all the hitching areas were filled with horses. The people had gotten the message! Their curiosity about the North Americans had been kindled. Mr. Glazner's publicity had been very effective, for the mountaineers were waiting for us.

I looked at my friend, missionary Dan Carrol, and said, "Dan, I'm so stiff, I don't know if I can get off of this pony." My bedroll was tied behind. In one hand I had the reigns and a rod and reel; in the other, I had a 410 single barrel shot gun we had taken in case we encountered some varmint, or maybe a quail or two. There I was, "Cowboy Glaze," so stiff I could not get off my horse. I said, "Dan, do you think you can get off and help me?" "Sure," he said, and as he swung off, his saddle loosened, and down he went. He landed flat on his back, one foot in the air hung in his stirrup. The Argentine cowboys cheered and applauded. That was our North American auspicious entry! The patient mountain pony turned and looked at Dan as he was lying there. An amazed pony viewed a flattened North American missionary!

Mr. Glazner came to the rescue. He helped Dan up and helped me down. Then he called the mountaineers to gather around. There were a number of men and boys that

4

assembled, but no women and girls. Julio Diaz, the national professor, preached a most powerful and relevant sermon. And incidentally, we had prepared a quartet back at camp. I am sure that Dr. Yarborough, our music director today, would have enjoyed hearing our "beautiful rendition." Also, I am sure that it was the first time any of that congregation had ever heard such disharmony in their lives! But, nevertheless, they listened. I still stand amazed at how God's Spirit moved, allowing his truth to shine through our humanity and frailty. That Sunday Julio preached a most powerful sermon on the "prodigal son."

He'd scarcely finished, when a man hurriedly came forward. He introduced himself. He was the mayor. He said, "Would you go to my house and have a bit of cognac with me?" I quickly responded, "Would it be impolite to ask for a cup of coffee? We ran out back at camp, and a good, fresh cup would taste good." He said, "Fine." "And your friends?" Cowboy Dan said, "Coffee would be great!"

We went to one of the few houses in Yacanto and met his wife and family. In a few minutes, we were alone with the mayor in his small dining room. He looked at Julio, and said, "I've never heard a message like this in all of my life. Where have you been?" Then he said, "This morning my eldest son and I had a bitter argument. He left. I don't know where to find him. Why didn't you come sooner? When can you come back?" He pulled a key out of his pocket, and said, "The Padre comes once a year for Christmas Mass. I have the key to the chapel. If you will come back, I will open it and we'll have church inside, not outside. When can you come back?"

I remember walking out the door of that house and looking down the half block to the eating place and the general store. I saw a sign on the general store that said "Tome Coca Cola"—"Drink Coca Cola." And my eyes moved around to a little sign by the hitching shed that said, "Singer Sewing Machines Sold Here."

We were never able to go back. I've lost contact with Mr. Glazner. I don't know where he is. I'm sure God does. I have prayed many times that the truth of God shared those days with our Jewish philosopher friend might somehow burn itself deeply into his heart. He became active in the mission enterprise by promoting, organizing, introducing, and preparing the way for our Christian witness. Oh, the mayor has been removed several times over, for there have been political coups since then. No longer would the same one be there. The prodigal son? I don't know what happened to him. For you see, we went back to our tasks. We were short of personnel funds. Actually, there were so many needs and opportunities so much closer! We were never able to go back to Yacanto!

I've asked myself many times, "Lord, what could it have meant?" Yacanto is legion. Yacantos are found all over the world. They are small places in remote areas, and large cities with the masses of the people. Hungry, lonely people are out there waiting for a message. "Why have you waited so long?" "When can you come back?" "Here, I have the keys." "I'll open the door." "Come back and share with us the message." "It is the greatest news we have ever heard." Lift up your eyes and look unto the harvest. The world is there, not simply statistics. It's Mr. Glazner and Juan; it's the mayor and his son. And God is at work, calling his own to look to the fields.

At the same time, the call of God includes *PRAYER*. "Pray ye the father that he will send his laborers into the field." This is intercessory prayer; this is transforming prayer that comes, not in changing God and his purpose, but that which in a powerful and dynamic way changes those who are willing to pray. "Beseech the Father," "pray." This is not a prayer of a tranquil mystical experience. It is not the prayer of one sitting in some quiet garden of meditation. It is a disturbing prayer. It is a prayer that comes in and tugs at your heart. It is a prayer that causes one to break from the ordinary, daily task. It is a break with one's family. It is a prayer that leads to going. As a Catholic missionary once said, "You'll go to a place where you are not wanted and not known, and you'll stay until you are wanted and loved. Then you will leave, and go someplace else to share the news of Jesus Christ." The call of God involves prayer.

As you look, and as you pray, the third mission imperative comes into focus: going, as you go, preach the gospel to
all creatures. As you go, "make disciples of all people." "All
power is given to me in heaven and earth." This morning
try to feel the heartbeat of Matthew and Mark. Persecution
had broken on the small Christian community. Under the
leadership of the Spirit, they looked back at the words, the
life, and the inspiration of the Master. They realized that the
going, the scattering, had already begun. The question was
not one of going! They were being scattered into a world
desperately in need. The urgency was to proclaim the truth,
and disciple the people!

Why does one go and proclaim the gospel? I think Keith
Parks expressed it very well several years ago. He had
wondered why his wife had packed the ceramic Christmas nativity scene as they went to Indonesia as missionaries. The first Christmas there, she unpacked it and set
it up. That day some Moslem women, some friends, came
to visit. When they saw the nativity scene, they asked,
"What does this mean?" Keith said his son, about five, was
playing on the floor with a little car. Seemingly he was not
listening. Mrs. Parks shared the significance of the nativity
scene and of the Christ event. Later, after the women left,
the son, as he continued to drive his little car, said,
"Mommy, tell me the story again." She said: "But son, you
understood it, you heard me." The little boy said, "Yes, but
I want to hear it in my language." Why does the missionary go? He goes so that a world can hear—in their
language—the wonderful message of Christmas, of Jesus,
of salvation.

How do you go? I cannot help but think of John's account
of one of the resurrection appearances. The fearful apostles
were behind locked doors. John reports that it was the same
day, that evening being the first day of the week, when
Jesus appeared and said, "Peace be unto you. As the Father
hath sent me, even so send I you" (John 20:21). When he
had said this, he breathed upon them and said, "Receive ye
the power of the Holy Ghost." Just as Jesus was sent out by
the Father, so he sends his own.

How was Jesus sent? How did he come? Jesus came as presence. He came as confirmation. He did not come as a conquering military hero that would bend history to his will through physical or material power. He came as the suffering servant. How did the disciples recognize Jesus Christ that day? They recognized him by the prints of the nails in his hands and the wound in his side. They recognized him as the Suffering Servant. Remember, we today, the church, the people of God, are the presence of Christ in this world. The world will never be bent by the power of the material, even the dollar! Nor will it be bent by the power of our own forcefulness. The world will be bent when the church becomes the suffering servant. When the church in compassion, is willing to be, and to do that which God would have done. Not until the church can be identified by the signs of Christ's suffering will there be the power that is so desperately longed for.

How does the missionary go? He goes, sent out in the spirit of Christ. "As the father has sent me, even so send I you." And he goes empowered with the strange and mysterious presence of the Holy Spirit. Even by means of a long night of dialogue on the road to Yacanto. Even through a Jewish agnostic, who became an instrument that opened the door of God's proclamation. He was the one that knew the people and could invite them to an open air meeting. How do you go? You go in the Spirit of Christ, and you go to all the world.

You go to a world that in many ways is hostile. You go to hard places. You will learn a new definition of success. It will not be the contemporary material success of the typical North American pastor. You will learn that statistically, there can be successful failures. You will go to places, and bury your life, and share it too. You will plow, and sow; however, you may not always experience the joy of the reaping. You will go to dangerous places, and you will go to strange places, with strange languages. You too, will probably hear that which I heard our first Christmas in Argentina, "Oh Lord, help our missionary. He has so much to say, and can't say it." Nevertheless, you will find a responsiveness. You will find that there is a victory. You will have the joy of seeing people born into the Kingdom of God. You will see growth and the spread of his kingdom, and that is a joy all its own.

Through it all Jesus has said, "Lo, I am with you always." Look and see the people. Pray that the father will send those that he sets apart; those that are appointed by the church, the fellowship, to go. In going, share the truth of Christ with the world.

It was a short term missionary that returned home. He had taken many slides, and in his report to the Brotherhood meeting, he saved for the last the slide that meant the most to him. Before he flashed it on the screen, he said, "I need to give you the background. It was early morning of my last day in Latin America. I woke about 4:00 am. I began to hear the stirrings of the city as the morning tasks began. It was still dark. Without a guide, I got up and dressed, took my camera, and went down to the entrance of the hotel to watch the early morning traffic. The dim street lights were still on, and I watched the people hurrying by." "Then," he said, "I caught the smell of freshly baked bread. I walked to the corner and then half a block down the street. There it was: a beautiful little family bakery. From the light inside the window, I saw those big rolls of bread: German bread, French bread, small loaves, different styles of bread." "So," he said, "I walked in just to savor the smell and to look at the attractive display. It was then I took my favorite picture.

"As I turned, etched against the blackness of that early morning darkness, bathed in the soft lift of the glow coming from the window of the bakery, I saw a little girl, about eleven years old, dirty and ragged. Her nose was pressed against the glass. She was looking at the bread inside. I took her picture." And with that he flashed the slide on the screen for his well-fed Baptist men.

Suddenly one of the men said, "John, what did you do?" John paused to respond: "At that moment I could feel the weight of the coins that had been in my pocket. I could almost hear the rustle of the bills of my currency. I had enough money in my pocket to buy all of the bread in the show window. I could have given that little girl enough to eat for days. What did I do? I took her picture!"

Do you get the picture? Lift up your eyes and *look* upon the harvest. *Pray* that the Lord of Harvest will send his laborers to his field. *Going, make disciples;* proclaim the truth to a world that is lost and in darkness. Be sure you get the picture.

A. Jack Glaze, Jr., has been the Chester L. Quarles Professor of Christian Missions and World Religions since 1985. From 1980–1985 he headed the Department of Religion and Philosophy at Mississippi College, after serving 27 years with the Foreign Mission Board in Argentina, where for 9 years he was president of International Baptist Theological Seminary. A graduate of Mississippi College (B.A.), and Southern Seminary (B.D., Ph.D.), Dr. Glaze is the author of "Jonah" in The Broadman Bible Commentary and numerous other works in English and Spanish.

The Christian As A Debtor

R. E. GLAZE, JR.

The first time I had the privilege of speaking in the seminary chapel service here was thirty-three years ago this spring. For you rookies on the faculty, I have good news and bad news. The good news is that it's always an honor to have the privilege of speaking to colleagues and students. The bad news is that, even after thirty-three years, it doesn't get any easier.

Our subject for the morning is "The Christian As A Debtor." No person, so far as I know, likes to be in debt. Unpaid bills can be like a weight around the neck that brings suffering and hurts our influence. Debts can take away the joy of living. I'm referring in the above statements to financial debts. There are debts, however, of a spiritual nature growing out of the fact that we have been redeemed by the blood of Christ. This places us in a state or condition of indebtedness.

In the book of Romans, Paul mentioned five of these debts. Unless we recognize these debts and are discharging them according to the will of Christ, we find that our lives are hurt far more even than in failure to discharge our financial obligations. Unless we engage in discharging these spiritual debts, our lives are choked, our influence is hindered, and the vibrant joy of victorious Christian living is absent.

All of these debts that we owe to Christ are expressed by Paul in relation to others and in relation to one's daily Christian living. Of course we are indebted to Christ because of what he has done for us. Nevertheless, we can express our

11

indebtedness to Christ only as we accept our obligation to live as he would have us to live and minister to others in his name. May we look now at the five areas of indebtedness that Paul mentions in the book of Romans.

THE CHRISTIAN IS A DEBTOR WHO IS OBLIGATED TO LIVE A NEW WAY OF LIFE

The first debt that I would mention is that we are indebted to live according to a new way of life. In Romans 8:12–13, Paul wrote, "So then, brethren, we are debtors, not to the flesh, to live according to the flesh—for if you live according to the flesh you will die, but if by the Spirit you put to death the deeds of the body you will live."

Here is one of the paradoxes of the Christian life, and there are many paradoxes in the Christian faith; salvation is free in the sense that we can never earn it; it also is deliverance from bondage in sin and to freedom in Christ. We are set free from that which would destroy us. Jesus said, "If the Son therefore shall make you free, you shall be free indeed." But to be free in Christ does not mean that all relationships have been severed.

To be free in Christ does not mean that we are free from obligation. For having been delivered from the crushing bondage of sin, we become slaves of Christ. Here again is a paradox: just as we live by dying and receive by giving, so we become free by becoming slaves. When we become Christians, we become free from all that could destroy us, all that would crush us, all that would lead us to unhappiness and alienation from God and others. As Christians, we become slaves to Christ; we no longer serve the old master. Jesus said we could not serve two masters. He did not give the option of serving no master. He said, "You will serve one and hate the other." When Christ becomes our master, we are indebted to live in keeping with his will, thus a new way of life. We are to live according to the Spirit.

One of the famous contrasts drawn in the writings of Paul is the contrast between *kata pneuma* and *kata sarka*; that is, life according to the spirit and life according to the flesh. The life according to the flesh is the life that is lived as if God does not exist or at least has no claim upon us. To live according to the Spirit is to let the ego be superseded by Christ, to substitute the Christocentric life for the egocentric life. To live according to the Spirit is to live daily in that spirit of desiring to be led by the Holy Spirit, to live daily in the attitude expressed by Christ even in the Garden of Gethsemane, "Not my will, but yours be done."

When we become Christians, we are born from above; we are regenerated; we are transformed; we become new creatures in Christ Jesus. The new creature is indebted to a life in keeping with that new creaturehood given by God's grace.

THE CHRISTIAN IS A DEBTOR WHO IS OBLIGATED TO SHARE THE GOSPEL TO ALL PEOPLE

Not only are we debtors to a new way of life, we are debtors who owe the sharing of the gospel to all people regardless of race, culture, or station in life. Paul said in Romans 1:14–15, "I am a debtor both to the Greeks and to the barbarians both to the wise and to the foolish, so as much as in me is, I am ready to preach the gospel to you also who are in Rome."

As a Pharisee, Paul had sought to save himself. Paul had sought to do this through his zeal for the law and through his loyalty to the traditions of the fathers. If Paul could have earned peace with God, could have earned salvation through this method, Paul would not have felt such a sense of indebtedness. But Paul learned that something was missing in his life. He lacked that peace, that joy that he ought to have had, and he sought it by his own efforts. And yet, Paul found this to be utter failure. He was driven to despair.

Paul, with his zeal for what he understood to be the will of God, sought to earn his own salvation. Thus finally, as he became more and more zealous for the law, and became more and more fanatical in persecuting those who disagreed with him, Paul started on the road to Damascus. There Paul cried out, no longer asking, "What can I do? How can I deliver myself?" But he confessed, "O wretched man that I am, who can deliver me from this body of death?" And then he added, I think, to give us the answer, "Thanks be unto God who giveth us the victory in Christ Jesus, our Lord."

The moment Paul took his hands off, and stopped trying to create within himself that which would merit a right relationship with God, God came in to give him the answer. The moment Paul was willing to say not, "I can," but, "Who can?" the answer came—Jesus can! Paul accepted this answer and found a new way of life. His life was transformed. Paul recognized that he had found the fulfillment of Judaism in Christ; not by his own efforts, not because he had sought God, but because Christ had sought him.

Paul viewed salvation as an act of grace from beginning to end. It was God's grace that caused God to reach out to probe and convict the heart of one who was persecuting his church. Paul did not take that free gift and then seek to enjoy it by using it for himself. But out of gratitude for what God had done for him, Paul saw that he owed to Jesus Christ a debt that he could never pay. He knew that if God could reach out and seek the salvation of one who was persecuting his church, that God surely wanted the salvation of every human being on the face of the earth. For Paul could conceive of no one being more rebellious and being more unworthy of salvation than he had been.

As Paul looked at the grace of God and examined his own obligation to respond to that grace, he became convinced that God wanted the salvation of others, then he could, in part at least, be in the act of discharging that debt to Christ by witnessing to others. He realized that his witness and longing for the salvation of others ought to be in the same character as God's longing for the salvation of others. He recognized that God made no distinction. He realized that God's grace was sufficient for all. Therefore as Paul exam-

14

ined his own life and asked what should be central in it, he concluded, "I am a debtor. I am a debtor because of what God has done for me through his grace. Therefore, I must discharge this indebtedness by doing that which God wants me to do, by witnessing to others, by sharing the gospel, and by demonstrating that the gospel makes no distinction."

God makes no distinction; therefore, in recognizing his obligation to others because of what Christ had done for him, Paul concluded, "I can make no distinction." And so, he said, "I am a debtor to all men, whether they be barbarians or cultured Greeks, whether they be ignorant or educated, whether they be slave or free." Race, education, background; none of this had any meaning at all in terms of his obligation to preach the gospel to all men.

If we could get a real vision of what we were apart from Christ, and know that in spite of what we were God loved us and sought our redemption, then in response to God's grace, I think there would develop among our people attitudes that would eliminate completely the kind of racial prejudice that exists in our world today. Paul was a debtor to all because he was a debtor to Christ, and so are we debtors to all mankind.

THE CHRISTIAN IS A DEBTOR WHO IS OBLIGATED TO LOVE CONTINUALLY

The third debt that Paul mentioned is that we are debtors in the sense that we are to discharge continually our obligation to love others. In Romans 13:8, Paul said, "Owe no one anything except to love one another, for he who loves his neighbor has fulfilled the law." The obligation to love, unlike some debts, cannot be paid once for all. Even some Christian debts cannot be paid. Knowing a lost person, I feel a sense of obligation to go witness to that lost person. I bear witness to him. He does not accept. I bear witness again and he still has not responded. I bear witness a third time and he trusts Christ. Now I am no longer obligated to witness to him concerning trusting Christ for salvation; the initial conversion experience has been discharged.

When a person is sick I am obligated to minister to that person. But my indebtedness to minister to him as a person who is ill is discharged when he recovers and is restored to health. The debt of love, however, can never be discharged. For when I witness to that lost person and that lost person becomes a Christian, I am still obligated to continue loving him. I had loved him as one in need of God's salvation; now I should love him as a Christian brother with whom I desire to have fellowship. One of the terrible attitudes among many Christians over the years has been that there are people to whom we're willing to witness, and then once they've confessed Christ, we don't want to claim them as Christian brothers and admit them to our churches.

Love is one obligation that never reaches the finish line. How foolish it would be for a man to say to his wife, "I think I've loved you lately more than the average husband loves his wife. I've worked so hard at loving you that for the next month or two I'm just not going to love you. I feel like I've given you all the love I owe you." No! No true love relationship would be expressed in such attitudes as that. We must continue to love just as Christ continues to love us. Christ loves us when we love him and are dedicated to his service, but he continues to love us when we sin. When we grow indifferent, his love is constant. His love does not change because of our response. We as Christians are obligated to express that constant love, not only to him, but to others also.

If our love toward others fluctuates up and down, our love toward Christ also fluctuates. We cannot love him whom we have not seen apart from loving those around us whom we have seen. The recognition and living of this truth of continual obligation to love will do more than anything else to build Christian lives and enable us to reflect Christ in daily living. First Peter 4:8 says, "Above all hold unfailing your love for one another, since love covers a multitude of sins."

THE CHRISTIAN IS A DEBTOR WHO IS OBLIGATED TO HELP WEAKER FELLOW-CHRISTIANS

Paul said that we are indebted also to our weaker fellow-Christians. It's so easy sometimes for us to get filled with pride, to look upon weak Christians as just surplus baggage to be carried by our church; but that's not the way Christ looks at them. That's not the way Paul viewed the weak. Paul said in Romans 15:1–2, "We who are strong ought to bear with the failings of the weak, and not to please ourselves, let each of us please his neighbor for his good, to edify him." Paul made this statement in relation to some specific problems of his day. But the principles are just as applicable to us as they were to the Romans to whom Paul wrote.

We're responsible not only for a love and concern that gives to us an evangelistic enthusiasm for those lost, we're responsible for loving and nurturing those who believe. We should help them to become effective in the work of Christ and to become vibrant and happy Christians.

Wherever there is an unhappy Christian, wherever there is one who is not optimistic and joyful in his Christian life; something has gone wrong. Now I do not mean to imply that the Christian life does not have its problems; it does. I do not mean to imply that there are never times when we may struggle and become discouraged. These times come not because of the weakness of Christ, but because of our own humanity. The life of the Christian never has been promised to be a life free from hurt, toil, tragedy, and hardship. Yet we need to help the weaker Christians, and we in turn need to be helped by others when we are weak.

We all are weak at times and we need to know that underneath all of our weaknesses there is that ever-sustaining power of Christ. He does not remove our problems in every case but always gives us grace to live through those problems and to be faithful to Christ in spite of the problems. So as we look about us, we see those who are hurting, those who are weak, those who have stumbled, and those who have been overtaken in sin. We have a debt to them because Christ came to us in our weakness.

THE CHRISTIAN IS A DEBTOR WHO IS OBLIGATED TO THOSE WHO HAVE GIVEN US THE GOSPEL AND NURTURED OUR CHRISTIAN GROWTH

Last of all, we would mention that we are debtors to those who have given us the gospel and nurtured our growth in Christian ministry. Paul said in Romans 15:26–28, "For Macedonia and Achaia have been pleased to make some contribution to the poor among the saints of Jerusalem; they were pleased to do it, and indeed they are in debt to them, for if the Gentiles have come to share in their spiritual blessings, they ought also to be of service to them in material blessings." Again, Paul is dealing with a specific situation, but there is an eternal principle here and that is that we are indebted to those who have made it possible for us in our Christian pilgrimage to be where we are. We today should remember our indebtedness to those who have given us the gospel.

We're indebted to the Old Testament Scriptures. We are indebted to those who were faithful. Many of the prophets paid with their lives for their faithfulness in proclaiming the Word of God. We are indebted to those who had hope and faith in the coming of the Messiah and kept that Messianic hope alive. We are indebted to the people of the Old Testament because they laid the foundation for our faith in Christ. The Jews did give to us the gospel. Paul was reminding the people in Rome that, while the Jews as a nation rejected Christ, they had given them the Scriptures, and it was they who first proclaimed the gospel. They broke asunder the bonds of narrow Judaism to bring the gospel to the Gentile world.

We today should remember our indebtedness to those who have given us the gospel. Oh, what a debt we owe to our parents who loved us and told us about Christ, and nurtured us in our early Christian growth. We owe a debt and an obligation to our churches. There's a small church in a rural area in Cullman, Alabama, that had many weaknesses. Yet it was at that church where some of my early concepts of Christ were formed that have lasted for a lifetime. I remember men, some of whom had not finished high school, who taught Sunday School classes that I sat in. I am indebted to them.

We are indebted to those who have labored under extreme difficulties in order to give us God's Word. Among these are Bible translators who paid with their lives for giving the Bible to the people in a language they could understand. We are indebted even to those monks who during the dark ages sat in their cells and copied Scripture, preserved Scripture, and brought it down to us. Maybe they should have been more evangelistic—that's beside the point as far as our indebtedness is concerned. We're indebted to the fact that they preserved the Scriptures and passed them on to us.

We're indebted to those who died under Nero. We're indebted to those who died under Domitian. We're indebted to those who died under the Spanish Inquisition. We're indebted to Anabaptists and others who died for their faith that we might have the faith we know today.

We who labor here at the seminary, both students and professors, have a debt that we ought to be paying continually to those who had a part in bringing this institution to where it is today. We like to refer to the institution as the School of Providence and Prayer. New Orleans Baptist Seminary *is* an institution of Providence and Prayer.

I'm afraid that sometimes we forget one aspect of this. We look at our buildings; we look at what we have today; we look at the enrollment; and we say all of this came to be because there were those who loved this school enough to pray for it; and thus, God in his providence answered their prayers and blessed this school. But there's another dimension that I think is often overlooked. There were days so dark in the background of this institution that professors did not have food for their children and seminary students did not have food for their families. When one would go out to preach and food would be given; this would be donated to the cafeteria where it would be pooled for all. For weeks at a time, parents, both students and faculty, would go eat in the cafeteria because there was no food at home.

For professors and students to keep this institution alive by going through that, they had to pray for themselves, not just for the institution. They had to pray to God for grace to endure this hardship, for grace to keep on keeping on. This school is a school of providence and prayer, not only because the school has grown, but because men and women, both among faculty and student body, so bathed their lives in prayer and so felt a nearness and a strength from God that they were able to stay at a task so difficult that it's hard for us to imagine.

I owe a debt to this institution because I soon will have spent thirty years here in addition to my years as a student. I owe a debt because of what I received here in training. I owe a debt to this school and those who have gone before me, because out of their sacrifice I have had joy, and by comparison, very few struggles such as they had. We would be less than ingrates, all of us, if we did not feel a debt to those who have gone before.

How can we pay that debt? Not like a church I served in Tennessee. My first experience as a pastor came while teaching senior high school science and serving two half-time churches, one in north Alabama and one in south Tennessee. After a year, I resigned the Alabama church and left for the seminary in Louisville. I continued to return to the Tennessee church two Sundays per month for two years. We needed a new building in the Tennessee church. We were ready to start the new building on Monday morning. When I got back two weeks later, nothing had been done. I found out later that a group of people had refused to let the work begin. They said, "We owe it to our fathers not to let the church that they built be torn down." That was not the way to pay the debt. The way to pay the debt was to sacrifice as their fathers had sacrificed in order to build the present church. They could pay that debt only by building a greater and better church.

And so it is that we can pay our debt here at the seminary. To those who have gone before us and given us this institution, we can repay by building on their foundation, by erecting a greater superstructure, by building on what they did, and going forward. We must make this school greater than the school they knew. They sacrificed to make it greater than what it had been. And so, as students, you can pay the debt by taking advantage of the greater opportunities of learning: the enlarged curriculum, the more efficient library that we have for doing the work, a better staffed faculty, and a better staffed administration. All of this has created for you an atmosphere of learning and the tools with which to learn.

You are indebted to those who went before, and you can pay that debt as you build your own life in ministry. To come to a school that has been built upon foundations laid by those who made great sacrifice and not give it your best is to be an ingrate, not only toward them, but toward the Lord Jesus Christ. To use your opportunities here for preparation to go out and witness more effectively is to express your gratitude in the highest way possible. Also, we as faculty members have an obligation to them to do a better job than former faculty members did because we have greater opportunities, greater facilities, and greater privileges. May we bow our heard now for prayer.

R. E. Glaze, Jr., Emeritus Professor of New Testament and Greek, taught at the New Orleans Baptist Theological Seminary from June 1956 until May 1988. Prior to this, he was Associate Professor of Bible at Louisiana Baptist College and served as pastor of churches in Alabama, Tennessee, Indiana, and Louisiana. He is author of *No Easy Salvation* and co-authored *Interpreting the New Testament*, as well as author of several articles for the *Biblical Illustrator, The Theological Educator,* and other periodicals. He holds the B.S. degree from Samford University, the B.D. degree from Southern Baptist Theological Seminary, and the Th.D. degree from New Orleans Baptist Theological Seminary and additional study at Princeton Seminary and Union Theological Seminary in New York.

The Larger Call Of Missions

BOB SIMMONS

Isaiah 49:1–6

It's a thrill for me to be here today to bring this missionary message. When the opportunity first came for me to come here to teach missions, I wasn't sure whether that was what the Lord wanted me to do. But since it worked out that way, I have found the subject of missions to be a constant thrill. I have been so very pleased that the Lord has led in this direction. I have not felt a bit like the two old folks I heard about one time who were sitting out on the old home place on the front porch. The old man, wrinkled and gray, was sitting there rocking with his wife of five decades. He looked over at her and saw her nose was almost touching her chin. She was almost deaf. Then he thought about all those five boys that she had given him, raised so beautifully, and sent out into the world. So in deep emotion he said to her, "Momma, I want you to know I'm proud of you." She turned and looked at him and said, "Daddy, I want you to know I'm tired of you too." There's not been one day in the studies here that I have been in the least tired of the message of missions. I'm grateful to have the opportunity to speak to you today about missions. I'm grateful for your interest.

Would you turn with me to Isaiah 49. We're going to read after a while from that passage.

I know of a young man who graduated at last from Johns Hopkins Medical School with a major in thoracic surgery. He was such a fine student and surgeon that Johns Hopkins wanted him to be a teacher there. So they said to him, "John, we want you to teach here. We know you will have opportunities to do marvelous things. So go on out, look around, and see what you can find. We will do our best to match it." The young doctor did that. He came back to his home state and looked around. He found a medical group that wanted to give him a guaranteed $250,000 annual salary. A quarter of a million dollars! That surgeon is now a missionary, teaching as he would have at Johns Hopkins, operating as he would have in his native state, and both for a missionary salary. What would make somebody do that? What would make somebody turn his back on that kind of opportunity to fulfill all of his dreams just to go and teach and practice surgery in Nigeria as a Southern Baptist Convention Foreign Mission Board missionary?

Maybe part of the answer is found in a text like this one. Listen!

> Listen to me ye islands, hear this ye distant nations: Before I was born the Lord called me; from my birth he has made mention of my name. He made my mouth like a sharpened sword, in the shadow of his hand he hid me; he made me into a polished arrow and concealed me in his quiver. He said to me, "You are my servant, Israel, in whom I will display my splendor." But I said, "I have labored to no purpose; I have spent my strength in vain and for nothing. Yet what is due me is in the Lord's hand, and my reward is with my God." And now the Lord says—he who formed me in the womb to be his servant to bring Jacob back to him and gather Israel to himself, for I am honored in the eyes of the Lord and my God has been my strength— he says; It is too small a thing for you to be my servant to restore the tribes of Jacob and bring back those of Israel I have kept. I will also make you a light for the Gentiles, that you may bring my salvation to the ends of the earth (Isaiah 49:1–6).

What a passage! It's found in a book I don't understand too well. I confess I walk through strange territory when I walk through Isaiah. It certainly is not my major, my expertise, at all. I don't really know in this one of four servant songs, as they say, whether the servant is Israel, in whole or in part, or whether it is Isaiah, or whether it is the Messiah. I've read and heard all three. I don't really know.

But I think the passage is applicable to my heart and my thoughts this morning. If it's Israel, we know ourselves that the church, the new Israel, is the instrument of God for the reaching of the world with the Gospel. If the church will go then some*one* must go. If it's Isaiah? Oh, I understand Isaiah. I know what it is to hear, "Who will go for me?" And what it is to say, "Send me." If it is the Messiah, I remember Jesus said, "As the Father has sent Me, so send I you." I hear, I hope correctly, the text as it says to me, "The task that the Lord has for you makes every other job a task too small. Life has no place so large, life has no responsibility so great, life has no dream so challenging but that it shrinks into a task too small when the Lord has something else for you to do."

My question is HOW? How did God say this to Isaiah? I've wondered so long. How did the Lord speak to Isaiah? I've wondered, did the Lord give to Isaiah an inspired ear so that he could hear something others could not hear? Did the Lord give to Isaiah inspired eyes so that he could see something that others did not see and translate it into some definite words and message? Or was it an inspired heart? I don't know. I guess I'll never know. I do know some ways in which the Lord has spoken to people down through the years to say, "I have a task for you that makes every other task too small."

SOMETIMES HE SPEAKS THROUGH KNOWLEDGE

In the last part of the eighteenth century, there was a young man named William Carey. He had been a poor boy. He was an apprentice to a cobbler. Early he married a girl who could not even read. He left the Anglican Church and became a Baptist. Soon he became a bi-vocational Baptist preacher. But, oh, did he have curiosity! His mind was like a sponge, a magnet. He wanted all the knowledge he could get. So he read all about Captain Cook's voyages; and he read Guthrey's Geographical Grammar. He learned all about the languages, and peoples, and customs of the world. The more he learned, the more he saw the need to reach a world for Jesus Christ. He went out as one of the first Baptist missionaries, from the first society that had as its goal the reaching of a lost world for Jesus Christ. Because he just learned, he learned. Everything he learned, he kept. Everything he learned, he put on that map on the wall before him. Everything he learned about the customs of the world told him that people everywhere without Christ were lost. Sometimes, also, the Lord uses what we learn to say to us, "I want you to be a light to the nations." For you, then, the task that you have is a task too small.

We learn about the religions of the world. We learn about the Moslems, who five times a day pray towards Mecca. Eight hundred million of them! If we could line them all up around this world and let them pray all together at the same time toward Mecca, they would form a ring around this world thirteen times. Not one of them has any understanding that God loves him. Not one of them thinks he speaks to a god who cares what he does. Not one of them knows about a Savior whose love brought him into this world to give himself for that one's salvation.

We learn about the Hindus, who pray to their three hundred million gods without any understanding that the Lord wants to come into their lives and help them bear their burdens within a dark caste system. The more we learn, the more we know that God loves them and wants them to know of his love. God uses this knowledge to say, "Your job has become a task too small."

SOMETIMES HE EVEN SPEAKS THROUGH SERMONS

One of my great sorrows is that so many of you never did get to know Dr. Baker James Cauthen, long-time Executive Director of the Foreign Mission Board. He could stir peoples' hearts about missions like nobody else I've ever heard. I've heard him so many times, as he would stand and lift his arms, "If God does not tell you stay, then go!" I've never been able to say that exactly, and certainly not like he did.

Dr. Cauthen wasn't always a missionary. When he was born into this world a Texas boy, he had all the talents one could have for ministry. Everybody knew he was going to be a preacher, and a good one. And he was. He received his education in Texas and then went to Southwestern Baptist Theological Seminary to complete his education. While he was completing it, he became a pastor, a very fine one, there in Fort Worth, at the Polytechnic Baptist Church. He married an MK named Eloise Glass. But missions was not in his mind. Even though he was a part-time missions teacher on the Southwestern campus, he knew that missions was not for him. He had been invited to go to China to teach missions there, but missions was not for him. Once he thought it might be, and he went to talk about it with somebody so fine as W. T. Conner. Dr. Conner suggested that Cauthen's talents were too great to spend on the mission field. Cauthen could mean more to people who would be missionaries than he could ever mean in a smaller ministry any place in this world. Cauthen agreed.

A time came, however, when he began to wonder. It was 1938, when things got tough in China because of the Japanese. One night in Fort Worth, he heard that there was going to be a preacher at the Presbyterian Church, a man named Robert Speer. Speer was a Presbyterian missionary statesman who had written a book that Cauthen had read, entitled *The Finality of Jesus Christ*. Cauthen went to hear him. Robert Speer preached about the upper room, of all things, not about missions. His message was that when the Lord went up into the upper room he used a room that belonged to somebody else. The person who owned the house and the room had to give it to Jesus. It was still his room, and he'd get it back. But he had to give it to Jesus. Baker James Cauthen sat up in the balcony and heard that sermon. After it was over he went home, but not to sleep. He sat up with his Bible and he read those passages that say,

"Unless a seed falls to the ground and dies, it produces nothing," and "If one will follow Christ let him take up his cross and follow me," and "He that loses his life will save it." And on and on and on. Then he went to his wife and said, "Eloise, it's time to pray about missions." A sermon.

Adoniram Judson, the first Baptist foreign missionary sponsored by a Baptist society from our country, decided he was going to be a missionary after he *read* a sermon. It was a sermon I've read that doesn't move me at all. In fact I have a hard time reading it through. It was "The Star in the East," by Claudius Buchanan, an Englishman. But when Judson read it, he said, "I'm going to be the first American foreign missionary!"

On our last furlough I went to preach in a lovely church in Mississippi. It was a bad day. Did you ever have one like that? I didn't like anything about it. From the time I walked into the church, from the time I shook hands with the pastor, and all through my bad sermon (it was the worst sermon!) everything seemed wrong. It was a bad day. A few months later I received a letter from somebody in that church. She wrote something like, "I just thought you'd like to know that Dr. so-and-so and his wife went home after that service and decided that their local practice was a task too small." They are foreign missionaries now. God uses sermons, even bad ones.

SOMETIMES HE SPEAKS THROUGH CIRCUMSTANCES

Let me tell you what happened to me. We thought we were going to be missionaries a long time ago. It didn't work out. I became sick, and then our kids got too old. We were in the pastorate for a long time. We had even had a chance to go over and do some missionary work in the Philippines.

The pastorate was a challenge to me for so long. I loved it. And I loved it on a day when I went out visiting. I knocked on a door, and nobody was home. I took out a card to put in the door. I opened that screen door and was about to put my card in the door when I saw that there were three cards already there. I put mine there, too. I turned around and walked to my car. I could take you to the very spot. Suddenly I stopped right in the middle of the sidewalk and thought, "What's really the difference between the Poplar Springs Drive Baptist Church, the First Baptist Church, the Highland Baptist Church and my church—the Fifteenth Avenue Baptist Church?" At that moment I couldn't decide if there was any. I thought, standing right there, "You know, if I leave this church they'll be able to get a pastor soon. But there are a lot of places in this world where there just are no pastors or preachers." From that moment, because it was God's will, my job seemed a task too small.

The Foreign Mission Board accepted us and we went overseas. We stopped in Japan to see our friends, the Calcotes, on the way. I just couldn't wait to get out there and meet all those folks in Hong Kong with whom I'd be serving. I was walking around the house in Japan following Gena Calcote, our hostess. I was just following her around so excited I didn't know what to do. I said to Gena, "Gena, you know what I'm doing now is just a lot more important than what I was doing before." Gena put her pan down, turned around and looked me right in the eye, and said, "Bobby, that is not so!! If all those folks weren't doing what they are supposed to be doing there you couldn't do what you're about to do over here." And she was right! But so was I—for me. For me, then, every other thing in this world was a task too small, because here was where God wanted me to be. Almost all the missionaries abroad look back to some little experience like mine that lets them see their task.

If you take all the Baptist preachers and their wives, about 70,000 of them probably, divide them into the population of the United States, you'll find there's about one Baptist preacher or wife for every 4,000 people in the United States. But if you divide our thousand Asian missionaries into the population of Asia, you'll find out that there is one missionary for every 2 million. If you divide all of our preachers and their wives into the total number of baptisms for the Southern Baptist Convention in any given year, you'll find that we each baptize about six. But if you divide all of our missionaries into baptisms abroad, you'll find that somehow each one is instrumental in some way in baptizing almost fifty people.

In Meridian we had a hard time trying to find out where we could put a new church. Where can you start a church when there are so many churches in some places? But there is a constant call from abroad for preachers and church starters.

God calls in so many ways. James McKay, the missionary who became a martyr in New Guinea, decided he was going to be a missionary before he was saved. One day his Sunday School teacher said to his class, "You've heard this letter from the Fiji Islands. Is there anybody in here who would give his life to be a missionary?" And James McKay said, "Yes." Alexander Chalmers was an engineer. He received a letter from his sister. She said, "They need doctors in Africa;" He said, "I'll be an engineer if they can use me." They tell me that David Livingstone was moved towards missions because he received a pamphlet that was sent to the wrong address.

I don't know how the Lord may speak to some among you. But hear me when I urge you, if God wants you to be a missionary, to say, "Yes."

The poet expressed my thoughts like this:

> I said, "Let me walk in the fields;"
> He said, "No, walk in the town."
> I said, "There are no flowers there;"
> He said, "No flowers but a crown."
>
> I said, "But the skies are black;
> There is nothing but noise and din."
> And he wept as he sent me back;
> "There is more," he said, "There is sin."
>
> I said, "But the air is thick,
> And the fogs are veiling the sun."

He answered, "Yet souls are sick,
  And souls in the dark undone."

I said, "I shall miss the light,
  And friends will miss me, they say."
He answered, "Choose tonight
  If *I* am to miss you, or they."

I pleaded for time to be given;
  He said, "Is it hard to decide?
It will not seem hard in heaven
  To have followed the steps of your guide."

I cast one look at the fields,
  Then set my face to the town;
He said, "My child, do you yield?
  Will you leave the flowers for the crown?"

Then into his hand went mine,
  And into my heart came he.
And now I walk in a light divine
  The path I had feared to see.

—George MacDonald

The theology of the poem may not be so good. But, oh, as one who knows a little about it, let me urge you to say "Yes" to God's call.

Bob E. Simmons is Associate Professor of Missions at New Orleans Baptist Theological Seminary. He graduated from Mississippi College (BA) and New Orleans Baptist Theological Seminary (B.D., Th.D.) He served pastorates in Louisiana and Mississippi from 1949 to 1974. He and his wife, Mary, became missionaries of the Foreign Mission Board in 1974. They served in Hong King and the Philippines.

The Other Side Of Calvary

JOE E. TRULL

Matthew 27:27–36

Have you ever seen the other side of Calvary?

Some years ago a minister who lived in Chicago, Illinois, commuted by railway train to his rural church. Every Sunday evening as he rode the express back to his home, the locomotive passed through a Chicago suburb called Calvary, Illinois.

Each week the conductor would cry, "Calvary—anybody for Calvary? Last call for Calvary." But the train never stopped, for no one ever got off at Calvary.

The reason was obvious. Peering out the side window, the minister viewed the village of Calvary—or what was left of it. Evidently the town had long ago been deserted, for all he could spy was a few empty buildings and an ancient dilapidated graveyard. There were no signs of life at Calvary.

And so it seems at the original Calvary lying outside the city walls of Jerusalem. No signs of life there. Only a place where criminals used to be executed. Today it is punctuated by tombstones, standing like limestone exclamation marks atop a hill that is now an ancient cemetery.

What really happened there? Why was Jesus of Nazareth crucified on that "green hill far away?" What makes his death so different?

Matthew records the event in his Gospel. After Jesus was nailed to the cross, the soldiers divided his meager garments. Then "they sat around and watched him as he hung there" (Matt. 27:36, LBT).

For centuries mankind, like those soldiers, has viewed that scene at Calvary and asked, "What does it mean? Why was Jesus executed? What did he mean by his final word from the cross, 'It is finished'?" (John 19:30).

Better for us to misunderstand any event in history than this one by which history itself numbers all events, B.C. or A.D. To really understand the cross we must see the other side of Calvary.

There are basically two ways to view the crucifixion of Christ and the events surrounding it.

First, we can look at Calvary objectively. With this analytical viewpoint we see the basic facts. What are they? A Roman cross—an instrument of death devised as a cruel means of executing capital offenders. An innocent victim— a man unjustly charged, illegally tried, impassively tortured, inscrutibly punished, excruciatingly crucified and horribly humiliated.

This is the view, for the most part, of literature, music and art. This objective point of view evokes our silent sympathy and sentiment. Both believer and agnostic agree, "The world stands condemned for putting to death an innocent man." Jesus was obviously mistreated and deserves our pity.

Yet there is another way to view Calvary. This is the subjective look. To see behind the objective facts, something not at first apparent to the eye. This subjective viewpoint is the singular look, the personal vantage point. To see the other side of Calvary is to grasp a revelation—that God is at work doing something unique and altogether unrepeatable in the death of Christ.

The subjective approach discovers that this is no ordinary death. Somehow in the mysterious movement of God in history an eternal sacrifice is being offered for the entire world. The cross is no longer a cloud shadowing man's depravity but a skylight revealing God's love.

If you have never seen this other side of Calvary, it's time to take another look at the cross. Time to gaze beyond the human drama on that Jerusalem hill to see that God is there, revealing our need and His response.

I. MAN'S SIN REQUIRED THE CROSS

The first revelation from the other side of Calvary is that man's sin required the cross. The skull-shaped hill is a reminder that the cross is God's response to man's sin.

In fact, sin is expressed at the cross. In a strange but true way, we actually perceive at Calvary the sinfulness of sin. The cross reveals what sin is and what sin does.

Here at Calvary sin comes out into the open. Golgotha reveals the height of hatred, the depth of depravity, and the breadth of brutality, for here we clearly witness the final results of man's alienation from God.

Never again can I say sin is unimportant. Never again can I euphemize sin, saying it is only an error, a mistake, or a slip of the conscience. When sin will seize the very Son of God and shamefully torture him to death, I now know what sin really is.

At Calvary sin is expressed in all of its hideousness. Sin is hatred. Sin is jealousy. Sin is pride. Sin is violence. Sin is deception. Sin is struggle for power. Sin is crucifying Jesus!

And everything on Golgotha that is morally offensive and repugnant appears in each week's issue of *Newsweek* and *Time*. If Jesus returned to earth today, we would crucify him again, for evil is still present in the human condition.

At Calvary then we see sin fully expressed. At the cross we can taste the fruit of sin, and it is rancid in our mouth.

Sin is also symbolized at the cross. That is another reason why man's sin required Golgotha.

Have you ever asked, "Who killed Jesus?" The question has precipitated much debate and produced many racial hostilities across the centuries. Some blame the Jews, and especially their religious leaders. Recounting the plots and plans of certain priests, scribes, and Pharisees, as well as their pressure and power-plays upon Pilate, many have concluded they were the real culprits.

Yet in actuality neither the Jewish nation of Jesus' day nor the present Jewish race can be blamed for the actions of a small minority who opposed Jesus. Certainly they did their best to eliminate the man who seemed to threaten their system. Indeed, the crowd did cry out, "His blood be on us and over our children" (Matt. 26:25). But these were not representative of the whole nation or the entire Hebrew race. We cannot scapegoat them.

If not the Jews, then certainly the Romans are responsible for Jesus' death. It is true that no criminal could be executed without the permission of Rome's representative. Pilate himself tried to evade that decision, even claiming to "wash his hands" of the whole matter (Matt. 26:24). In the end, however, "he delivered Him to be crucified" (Matt. 26:26).

It was Caesar's soldiers who carried out with consumate skill the crucifixion of Christ. Yet, to blame the occupying army for Jesus' death is to miss a significant revelation from the other side of Calvary.

Jesus himself said, "I lay down my life . . . No one takes it from me, but I lay it down of myself . . ." (John 10:17–18). Here then is the answer. If I can discover what caused Jesus to lay down his life, then I can know what, or who, killed Jesus.

"I am the good Shepherd; and I know my sheep . . . and I lay down my life for the sheep" (John 10:14–15). There it is. Jesus, the Son of God, laid down his life voluntarily for his sheep—for you and me. It was my sin that was symbolized at the cross. It was your transgression that nailed him to the tree. It was our iniquity that drove the nails into his hands and feet.

You have never seen the other side of Calvary until you realize you are responsible for his death. Your disobedience caused him to die, for when he laid down his life for his sheep, he died for you. "While we were still sinners, Christ died for us" (Romans 5:8).

Not only is sin expressed at the cross and symbolized there, but best of all sin is conquered at the cross. At Calvary man's sin problem is solved. This unique death of Jesus accomplished our salvation, "for Christ also suffered for sins, the just for the unjust, that He might bring us to God" (1 Peter 3:18).

Through his vicarious sacrifice, every person can be rescued from the penalty, power, and ultimately the very presence of sin. Christ suffered all the Hell I ever need to fear. Jesus was a divine substitute for my sin. He not only died for me, but he also died in my place.

Listen to the Apostle. "For he [God] made Him [Jesus] who knew no sin, to become sin for us, that we might become the righteousness of God in Him" (2 Cor. 5:21).

Out of the Civil War comes a story of an amazing sacrifice. Union soldiers captured a company of irregulars known as "bushwackers." Because they were guerilla fighters and not in uniform they were sentenced to be shot. One young man in the Union army touched his Commander on the arm and said, "Will you let me take the place of one of the condemned prisoners? I know him well. He has a large family that needs him badly. My parents are dead and I have no family. Let me take his punishment."

The surprised Union officer granted the request. Before the firing squad stepped Willie Lear in the place of his friend.

Today, if you visit the Missouri graveyard near the site of the military execution, you will find a memorial tombstone with these words inscribed:

> Sacred to the memory of Willie Lear
> He took my place

If a memorial could be erected on Golgotha's hill, it ought to read:

> Sacred to the memory of Jesus Christ
> He took my place

There is much about the death of Christ I do not fully comprehend, but this I know. Because of Jesus' sacrifice, my sins are forgiven, my sickness is cured, and I have eternal life.

> Amazing grace! how sweet the sound,
> That saved a wretch like me!

I once was lost, but now am found,
Was blind but now I see![1]

To see the other side of Calvary is to realize man's sin required the cross. The very sin so vividly expressed at the cross was also symbolized there for my sinfulness, and conquered there by the atoning sacrifice of Christ. To discover that truth is to perceive the revelation that "God was in Christ reconciling the world to himself . . ." (2 Cor. 5:19).

There is another major revelation at Calvary. It also requires the subjective focus to discern this deeper meaning of the cross.

To see the other side of Calvary is also to understand:

II. GOD'S SON CHOSE THE CROSS

Jesus climbed to the cross. It was not a bypath, an after thought, or a detour. Not something just to be endured, but a goal to be achieved. For Christ the way of the cross was a main road, a thoroughfare leading straight toward the will of God.

Christ chose the cross first, as his redemptive sacrifice for our salvation.

Calvary was the climax of Jesus' life. From the first beat of his heart, Calvary was Christ's divine imperative. He was born to die.

When John the Baptist's eyes first fell on the teacher from Nazareth, he cried out, "Behold! The Lamb of God who takes away the sin of the world!" (John 1:29).

This is the Gospel, the old, old story of which we never tire. The Scripture approaches the scene with hushed voice and holy hesitation.

The sky blackens as if some gigantic hand has eclipsed the sun. The earth heaves with cataclysmic pain. In the Temple, that heavy veil separating the holy of holies from the Court of Priests is torn from top to bottom. Lightening flashes above the Sea of Galilee to the East and thunder rolls across the plains of Jezreel.

The dying figure on the central cross raises his head as if to capture one last gasp of breath. "It is finished!" (John 19:30), he cries. And he dies.

What was finished? The redemptive plan of God by which all mankind could be saved. God's Son chose the cross as the sacrifice for our salvation.

The other side of the cross also visualizes another truth— Jesus Christ chose the cross as an expression of God's love. On that rocky prominence just outside Jerusalem's eastern gate God revealed His love. The cross is the love of God in action.

How do I know God loves me? Because Jesus Christ, God's Son, died for me on a Roman cross. "In this is love, not that we loved God, but that He loved us and sent His Son to be the propitiation for our sins" (1 John 4:10).

The apostle to the Gentiles wrote, "God was in Christ reconciling the world to Himself . . ." (2 Cor. 5:19).

If man's sin were the last word, the scene at Calvary would depress us to the point of suicide, and we Judas-like would perish. But man's miserable condition is not the concluding chapter of the drama. It is only the prelude.

The main movement, like the recurrent theme in a symphony, is the majestic overture of the love of God. When man did his worst, God responded with His best. "Where sin abounded, grace abounded much more" (Romans 5:20).

Come to the other side of Calvary and view the fullness of God's love. The death of Christ both reveals and fully expresses the love of God.

A third reason why Jesus chose the cross was as a way of life for his followers. One of the greatest challenges uttered by Jesus is recorded in all three Synoptic Gospels: "If anyone desires to come after Me, let him deny himself, and take up his cross daily, and follow Me" (Luke 9:23).

Paul picked up on this theme when he wrote, "I have been crucified with Christ; it is no longer I who live, but Christ who lives in me; and the life which I now live in the flesh I live by faith in the Son of God, who loved me and gave himself for me" (Gal. 2:20).

Here then is the principle, the standard by which life must be measured. Here is the goal, the prize, the laurel wreath of the Christian race. The cross is the way of life for all Christians to follow. But what does that mean?

Josephus in his history of the "Wars of the Jews" recorded an insurrection in Palestine around the year 6 A.D. Because of dissatisfaction with Archelaus, son of Herod the Great, and increasing hostility toward the Romans, a large group of Jews revolted and laid seige to the city of Jerusalem.

Quickly a Roman officer, Varus, brought from Antioch two legions and 1500 armed men to rescue the city. After quelling the revolution he captured those most guilty and ordered them crucified.

Following Roman custom, these 2000 insurrectionists were impaled on crosses erected every few hundred feet on a main travelled road outside the Joppa Gate. To teach all Israel a lesson in Caesar's law, the young revolutionaries' bodies were left hanging for weeks until the flesh had rotted and the buzzards had picked the bones clean and the skeletal remains lay bleaching in the Palestinian sun.[2]

Jesus and his disciples were young teenagers then. Undoubtedly they heard of the revolt and the humiliating death of these Jewish heroes. It is possible some of them even journeyed to Jerusalem to see the sight.

So when Jesus called his disciples to "take up their cross," it was not a beautiful bronze cross on a church steeple that crossed their mind. It was not a lovely gold cross about a young girl's neck they envisioned.

When Christ said "cross," all they could see was a dirty, bloody wooden cross on which a limp figure was dying.

Jesus was saying to his followers, "Remove from your mind all glorified ideas of importance, for if you choose to follow me, you must be willing to die a death like that!"

We cannot join Jesus in suffering for the salvation of the world, but we can identify with him in a life of self-sacrifice and service. Discipleship is a daily death. Death to self and sin. Living by the cross-principle means becoming a "Jesus-person." We live by dying. The cross was not only a sacrifice for our salvation and an expression of God's love, it continues to be the way of life for Christians to follow.

To see the other side of Calvary is to take a new look at the cross, to view Golgotha from a different vantage point. It is to discover beyond the objective facts the deeper meaning of the death of Christ—a revelation of man's need and God's response.

There is an interesting sequel to the story of the minister who rode the train each week back to Chicago. One Sunday night, as the conductor called out, "Calvary. Anybody for Calvary?", a man signaled and started gathering together his belongings.

The train stopped. The traveler detrained. Astonished, the minister again looked out his window and saw the same scene—a few old buildings and a deserted cemetery.

Why would anyone stop at Calvary? Then the weekend pastor realized he had never looked out the other side. Stepping across the aisle, he peered into the dusk to spy a revealing scene. High on a hill was a little house, with lights shining and smoke curling out of the chimney. On the front porch was a smiling wife and excited children welcoming their daddy home.

All of these years the minister had looked out of his train window and seen only one side of Calvary—the side where there was only darkness and death.

That evening he discovered the other side of Calvary— the side where there was light and life.

Have you seen both sides of Calvary? Not only the death he died, but also the life he gives.

How about it? Anybody for Calvary? Last call for Calvary!

NOTES

[1]Words by John Newton, 1779.

[2]Flavius Josephus, *Wars of the Jews*, Book II, Chapters 3–5

Joe E. Trull has been Associate Professor of Christian Ethics at New Orleans Baptist Theological Seminary since 1985. Prior to this he served as pastor of First Baptist Church of El Paso and other churches in Texas, Virginia and Oklahoma. A graduate of Oklahoma Baptist University (B.A.) and Southwestern Seminary (B.D., Th.D.), he has also authored *Forty Object Sermons for Children* and *Seven Last Words of the Risen Christ*.

A Door of Hope

JERRY BREAZEALE

Hosea 1–3, 11

Our God wants so desperately for us to know how much he loves us. Words are inadequate. Supremely, he showed us in the incarnation of his Son. But in the Old Testament, perhaps eight hundred years or so before the incarnation of his Son, he chose to describe himself in words that I would be afraid to use of God had he not used them first. For he is described for us in the prophecy of Hosea as the Father of disobedient children, as the husband of an unfaithful wife and as a door of hope in a valley of trouble.

You remember most of the story. God the Father, crying out from his own broken heart, saying, "What could I have done that I didn't do? When Israel was a child, then I loved him and called my Son out of Egypt, and as they called them, so they went from them. They sacrificed unto Balaam and burned incense to graven images. I taught Ephraim also to walk, taking them by their arms but they knew not that I healed them. I drew them with the cords of a man, with bands of love, and I was to them as they that take the yoke off their jaws, and I laid meat unto them."

God was the Father of disobedient children—stubborn, rebellious, self-willed, intense little boys. And when they fell, he lifted them up and brushed them off, and maybe did that motherly act of kissing them and making the hurts well. And things were better. As they tried to learn to walk, he took them by the hand and he led them, although they didn't know it. They were unconscious that it was he. Perhaps, they thought it was of themselves. But he knew that their footprints, as they learned to walk, were taking them farther and farther from him; farther and farther away from home. He begged them. He besought them, "Continue with me." The Father's love reached out.

It reminds you of another story: "This my son which was dead is alive." And it reminds of yet another story: That time when a hand reached down to you. You had stumbled. You had fallen, and that voice said, "Rise, child, I am your Father."

That little cameo is not the central one that you find in the book of Hosea, as most of you well know. The thrust of the first three chapters is based upon the story of a broken heart and a broken home. It has been said that Hosea learned about God's love where we all learn it best—in the crucible of human experience. He learned about God's broken heart in his own broken heart. He learned about God's love in his own frustrated, denied love.

You remember the story. Hosea met Gomer, fell in love with her and married her. It starts off like a good fairy tale, but sin is no part of a fairy tale; it is a part of the human condition. After the first few years, it seemed that a shadow of suspicion began to darken the mind of Hosea that Gomer was not being faithful to him. By the time the third child was born, that suspicion had been confirmed apparently, for he named that third child, "Not my child." He pled with his wife. He begged her to mend her ways, and he asked the older children to talk to their mother. They did, but she wouldn't hear. The Bible doesn't give all the details, but apparently she went from man to man until there came a day when she was desirable to no man. At last she was being sold on the village slave block. God said to Hosea: "Go down and buy her back, and take her as your wife." A man among us recoils in self-righteousness and hypocrisy and says: "Hosea was a sentimental fool; Gomer made her bed, he should have let her lie in it." But this isn't man's story; it's God's story. And God said: "I loved you."

The text says that Hosea took fifteen pieces of silver and a homer and a half of barley. I read in at least one commentary the suggestion that Hosea took fifteen pieces of silver— all he had—although the ransom price for a slave was thirty pieces of silver. He took fifteen and he took his seed grain for the next year, and he went down there. They laughed when he came. They mocked when they saw what he intended to do. But he took the totality of his possessions and exchanged it for this woman who had treated him like dirt! Remember, it is God's story. They may have laughed and mocked at Hosea that day, but they laughed and mocked even more when the bright Son of God was hanging on Calvary's cross and in the mid – afternoon darkness cried out, "My God, My God." Hosea may have indeed given all that he possessed to go and buy her back, but God gave heaven's brightest possession—Jesus Christ—to come into this world for rebels like you and like me. It is not man's story; it is God's story.

Who can imagine what was in the young man's heart as he said, "You come back home, and we will live through a period of purification, and you shall again be my wife and I shall be your husband." What is it, students? It is the story of the ages. It is God saying to sinful rebels: "Now, that you have drunk the drink of sin to the dregs, the bitter dregs in the bottom of the cup, come back home and I will be to you a Father and you will be my child." You wonder how Hosea could have sensed so much, so long before the cross. We on this side of the cross have greater insight, but Hosea sensed it.

A third little cameo I would share with you is found in the second chapter. "Therefore, behold I will allure her and bring her into the wilderness and speak comfortably unto her, and I will give her her vineyards from thence and the valley of Achor for a door of hope, and she shall sing there as in the days of her youth and as in a day when she came up out of the land of Egypt. I will give her the valley of Achor for a door of hope." Strange when you first look at it. Hosea now understood that sin was terrible and that sin must be punished. Hosea understood now the intensity and the immensity of God's love for him, but there was yet one thing that he had to learn. God said, "I will give you the valley of Achor for a door of hope." One writer says that Achor means trouble, or troubling. It is used three times in the Scripture. It is used once in the book of Joshua to describe the judgment that was meted out to Achan after he stole those robes and pieces of precious metal and hid them under the floor of his tent. It was there in the valley of Achor, or the valley of trouble, or troubling, that he and his family members were stoned.

It is mentioned a second time in Isaiah 65:10. There it is associated with Sharon as a place of rest and protection and prosperity. God says to his people: "I will give you the valley of Achor for a door of hope." A new note has emerged. There has been a message of judgment, yes! But, as is so strangely true all the way through this little prophecy of Hosea, God's judgment and God's love never seem to be very far apart.

Back in the eleventh chapter, from which I read a moment ago, when God takes us as little children, you hear the very heart-cry of God, "How can I give thee up, how can I make thee like the cities of the plain which have been destroyed." And then it is almost as though, in the stillness of infinity, you hear the heart of God break. God says, "I can't, I can't." All of that is in the balance; all of that is in the background. Now he gives this picture, this note of restoration, this note of renewal, this message of hope. Yea, it is a message to all those who are in the valley of troubling. There he will give you a door of hope.

The troubling was the judgment of Gomer. The troubling was the judgment for Israel as they were swept away into captivity. The valley of troubling had to be there. In the midst of the valley, there is always the door—the door of hope. I realize that we don't even use those two words together, ordinarily, unless we say, "I hope I don't have trouble." That is about the only way I can think of that we use those two words together. Hope and trouble, in some strange way, seem to be used together. Judgment had to come. Hosea knew that. He understood that his wife had to be bought back, just as God, in his infinite mercy, redeemed us when Jesus died on the cross. He bought us back not with silver and gold or perishable things, but with the Son of his love.

Who was it that linked the valley of Achor with the door of hope: I think it was God himself. God was with Hosea and Gomer there in the valley of trouble. Faber once said, "There is no place where earth's sorrows are more keenly felt than in heaven." Jesus took upon himself the aggregate of human sin. Could you take the suffering and the hurt in just one class today and put it all into one big wad of ugliness? It would be a frightful load. But what if you took the troubles and the hurts and the pains of all the world and massed them together, and then put them on the shoulders of that one who had not sinned but who had come in the likeness of sinful flesh. The valley is real enough. Most of us have been there. God cares. God cares like the Father cares about his disobedient children, like the husband cares about his disloyal wife. God cares. He shares with us in those experiences.

Creation was an act of love. It was an act of God's sovereignty, and renewed relations must also be the result of God's love. Maybe I can pull in a passage from John to say what I want to say better than I can say it otherwise. The Lord said on the night before the crucifixion: "Now is my soul troubled, and what shall I say. Shall I say, 'Father, save me from this hour'?" And then he answered himself, "No, for this reason I came into this very hour. Shall I say, 'Father, glorify thy name'?" And again before he could answer himself, there came the voice from God saying, "I have glorified it and I will glorify it again." And he set his face steadfastly toward the cross. "Now is my soul troubled!" You get the feeling that it is so sacred that you are afraid to touch it. But what was this turmoil of soul that Jesus experienced? I think in part, it must have been related to that great sin burden of the world that I spoke about just a moment ago. Did Jesus know, in his humanity, that he could bear it? I think there may have been a substantial question in his mind. Up to this point, in all of human history, who had ever known the aggregate of human sin? But he took it all. In the valley of troubling, his soul was troubled.

Now I am going to wrest a verse completely out of context. You professors just excuse me. We have our own valleys, and although I know the reference in Hosea is primarily to the valley that they were using as God's judgment or judgment upon Achan, or some other form of specific judgment, I also recognize that those valleys may not be just God's judgment upon us. Because parallel to the valley of Achor, there run a great many other valleys—of financial hardships, family breakups, and physical disabilities—and we find ourselves in one of them.

Am I being unfair to the total teaching of God's word to suggest that God says to us today: "I still will be your door of hope in the valley of trouble." I think I can say it. God loves his people. He hurts when we hurt. But we must remember also the corollary, and that is that he grieves when we sin. Do you remember when he came and found you—an adulterous, idolatrous rebel, being sold on Satan's slave block? God interposed and gave his Son to set us free, to bring us back, trash like we were. If he did that, is he not sufficient to provide you the strength for living through the days of the valley of trouble? Yes, for he is the door of hope at the end.

A final thing that I would suggest. God always seeks sinners in order to restore them. I suppose Gomer went back to Hosea. I suppose that one day that marriage was restored. But I also know that God found me in the valley. He restored a relationship, a relationship broken because of sin, because of my stubbornness and because of a multitude of things. But, in effect, what does he finally say when we meet his conditions? "Come home and you be to me a son and I will be to you a Father." Sin has no door of hope. Those who are just in the valley of sin don't find the door, but those who, in Jesus Christ, find themselves in the valley of troubling, also find the door of hope. He said it, didn't he—"I am the door." Where is your valley? Most of you have been there. Did you find the door? Did you come back to God like Gomer came back to Hosea and like Israel, ultimately, came to God after the captivity? Oh! How he loves you and me!! May we pray.

Lord, thank you for your matchless love. Would you send us away from this place with renewed consciousness of how

47

much you love us. And if like Gomer or the disobedient children, we have strayed away from you and gone in our selfish, self-willed ways, call us back even if it takes a valley of troubling. Renew and restore the relationship. Let that love that you have for us be manifested in our lives to other people—to our families and to our children, our fellow students, and fellow faculty members. Oh, Lord, the soul of our Master was troubled, and certainly we should ask no less. But in our valleys of troubling, would you always illuminate for us the door of hope through Christ Jesus our Lord, in whose name we pray, Amen.

Jerry Breazeale is professor of New Testament and Director of the School of Christian Training. He has been on the New Orleans Seminary faculty since 1976. Previously, he pastored churches in Natchez, MS, Raymond, MS, and Bogalusa, LA. He holds the B.A. from Mississippi College and the B.D., Th.M. and Th.D. degrees from New Orleans Baptist Theological Seminary.

Does It Do Any Good to Pray?

C. FERRIS JORDAN

Ask and it will be given to you, seek and you will find. Knock and it will be opened to you. For everyone who asks, receives; and he who seeks, finds; and to him who knocks, it will be opened. Or what man is there among you who if his son asks for bread, will give him a stone? Or if he asks for a fish, will he give him a serpent? If you, then, being evil, know how to give good gifts to your children, how much more will your Father who is in heaven give good things to those who ask him (Matthew 7:7–11).

As I thought about some scholars to whom I might turn who would help me gain some insight into this passage, I thought about one whom you may not have suspected— Mark Twain, by name. I found out that Mark Twain has a lot of insight into a lot of things and I discovered one of his characters, Huckleberry Finn, having some comments to offer about prayer. These were Huck's comments:

Miss Watson, she took me in the closet and prayed, but nothing come of it. She told me to pray every day and whatever I asked for I would get it. But it warn't so. I tried it. Once I got a fish-line, but no hooks. It warn't any good to me without hooks. I tried for the hooks three or four times, but somehow I couldn't make it work. By and by, one day, I asked Miss Watson to try for me, but she said I was a fool. She never told me why, and I couldn't make it out no way.

I set down one time back in the woods, and had a long think about it. I says to myself, if a body can get anything they pray for why don't Deacon Winn get back the money he lost on pork? Why can't the widow get back her silver snuffbox that was stole? Why can't Miss Watson fat up? No, I says to myself, there ain't nothin' in it.[1]

I suppose that there are a lot of folks in the world and some in our churches who would probably say "Amen" to Huck Finn. They tried it; it wasn't so; and they concluded that "there ain't nothin' to it." Some have prayed for health, and sickness has come. Some have prayed that a loved one would be spared, and death has come. Some have prayed for material things, but they haven't materialized. And so they have looked at the word of Jesus, "Ask and it will be given you, seek and you will find," and they have said as Huckleberry Finn, "There ain't nothin' to it."

Many of those who are bothered in this way about prayer are troubled not only because they don't understand the answers they have received or have not received, but also because they are living with the wrong concept of prayer. Some of those with whom we work, and perhaps some of us in this place, from time to time wonder about what prayer really is after all. For some folks in our world, prayer is just a mere superstition. It's some kind of mumbling to one's self under the delusion of addressing deity. For other people in our world prayer is a kind of black magic. It's like rubbing an ecclesiastical Aladdin's lamp. As a result, some heavenly genie is supposed to come and manipulate the world and give one whatever he desires. Others probably think prayer is something like self communication. It is some kind of psychological form of talking to yourself, and in the process, getting in touch with some things deep in your being that were there all the time.

Persons who are wrestling with prayer and living with those kinds of concepts would naturally say "Amen" to what Huck Finn said. But as I understand it from reading the Scripture, prayer is conversing with God. Prayer is family talk. Prayer is frank, open, intimate conversation with the one whom we in Christ have come to know as our Heavenly Father. And I am sure that if I asked this chapel congregation, "Is there any value in prayer, does it really do any good to pray?"—that from this group there would come a resounding, "Yes." We would say, "Jesus prayed very effectively; Jesus taught us to pray in his model prayer. He showed us the spirit that ought to be ours when we pray. He showed us the ingredients that ought to be present when we pray." Yes, indeed, prayer is important. There is value in prayer. I think that for us, as well as for those with whom we may work from time to time in the church, it may be helpful to think together this morning about why prayer really is so important.

PRAYER PUTS US IN TOUCH WITH GOD

I suggest to us first of all that prayer is valuable, because prayer puts us in touch with God. When I truly pray in the spirit in which I have been taught to pray, I do so believing in God. I come to him as my Heavenly Father. I center my attention on him. I express reverence toward him. I adore him. I seek to know his will above anything else. I humble myself before him. I am putting myself in a position to receive him and his direction for my life rather than to be ignoring him or rebelling against him. And in the process of doing those things and coming in that kind of attitude I indeed can get in touch with God. In the midst of a world of great uncertainty, I am in touch with him who is certain. In the midst of a world where things are passing away, I am in touch with the one who is eternal. In the midst of much confusion that is often a part of my life, I am in touch with him who can give me perspective. Those things make prayer very important in my life. As I think of these things, I am reminded of Habakkuk. You will recall Habakkuk's experience. In the first chapter we have the record of his being so troubled because God appeared to be so inactive and so unaware of the evil that was present among his people. Habakkuk expressed all of that to God in that frank, open kind of way that I have been talking about. God responded, you remember, by saying to Habakkuk, "I am doing things that you wouldn't believe if you could see it." God began to tell him of his plan concerning Chaldea. Then you remember how Habakkuk responded with doubts and with great frustration that God would use a wicked nation to accomplish his purposes among his own people. But then you may also recall that Habakkuk decided, "I will wait and watch in faith." And before the book is over, because he had been in touch with God, because he had gained God's perspective on things, he issued a statement of triumphant faith.

> Although the fig tree shall not blossom, neither shall fruit be on the vines, though the yield of the olives should fail, and the fields produce no food, though the flocks should be cut off from the fold and there be no cattle in the stalls, yet I will rejoice in the Lord, I will joy in the God of my salvation. The Lord God is my strength (Habakkuk 3:17–18).

Arthur H. Clough, a lesser known poet in England in the nineteenth century, lived through very turbulent times. He observed the havoc wrecked on the world by many of his contemporaries, but he came to an experience of faith when he wrote these lines:

> It fortifies my soul to know
> That though I perish, Truth is so;
> That howsoe'er I stray and range
> Whate'er I do, thou dost not change;
> I steadier step when I recall
> That, if I slip, Thou dost not fall.

Prayer helps us keep that kind of perspective. Sometimes trouble shakes us as if we were in some kind of sieve.

Earth's events jolt us like an earthquake. Through prayer we get in touch with God. We come to know him better. In the process of prayer, we develop our confidence that he knows us and cares about us. In our contact with him we find a semblance of order in the midst of life's disorder. Prayer is important because it puts us in touch with God.

PRAYER NOURISHES GOD'S LIFE IN US

I think another insight that we need is that prayer is valuable because it is one way that God nourishes his life in me. When I became a Christian, I went through that experience the Bible calls being born again. In the process of the new birth, God gave me a new nature, a new nature directed toward godliness. I now have the responsibility of choosing to neglect or to nurture that nature. I can neglect it and grieve the Holy Spirit greatly, or I can cooperate with the Holy Spirit of God who lives within me and nourish the life that God has given to me. I believe that prayer is one of the ways through which God works in my life to nourish in me his kind of life. I pray and God seems to delay. In the process, he is teaching me patience. I raise questions with him in prayer, and God remains silent. In the process he is teaching me that peace comes not in having the answers, but in having his presence. I pray for his intervention and he seems not to intervene. He seems to remain inactive. In so doing, he has a way of teaching me that the real way to travel in life is the way that says, "not my will, but thine be done." I pray and talk to him about daily provision for my life, and in the process of talking to him about my daily bread, he is teaching me that I am frail and he is very strong. I am very dependent and he is very adequate. I pray for those who may have done me wrong, and in the process of prayer, God is nurturing forgiveness in me. I confess to him my perplexity and my confusion, and he teaches me in the process something about acceptance of my circumstances.

I like Winston Pearce's observation about prayer. He said, "The highest realm of prayer is when and where a person comes day after day to practice the presence of God. It is here that the will and way of God become our will and way. Here we come not to seek gifts, but to be; not to receive, but to become."[2] And so as God is helping you to be, as he is helping you to become, he is nurturing his life in you.

PRAYER OPENS LOCKED DOORS

One final thought—prayer is very valuable to us because prayer does indeed open some of the locked doors of life. Charles Allen, the renowned Methodist minister, spoke of a man who went through a certain ritual each day as a part of his spiritual discipline. This man had a way of putting his key ring into one of his shoes every night as he went to bed. The next morning he got up, dressed, and the last thing he did was put on that shoe and take out the key ring. He would then talk with the Lord about it, and the communication would go something like this: "Lord, today I will encounter certain doors that are locked that I will unlock with these keys. Help me to remember as I go through the day today that there is a key to every situation. Help me never to surrender to life's closed doors. Instead, help me to use the keys on the key ring of prayer until I have found the right key."[3] I do believe the scripture which says, "The things which are impossible with men, are possible with God" (Luke 18:27).

I do believe the Bible when it says, "If thou canst believe, all things are possible to him that believeth" (Mark 9:23). And so I must say to myself and to you this morning that with God nothing is ever hopeless. He may not change some of the circumstances I pray to him about as I hoped he would. He may not respond with some of the affirmative answers I had desired; but as I pray, God is at work. And when God is at work, nothing is hopeless. I am communing with him in an attitude of reverence. When I am before him in an attitude of submission, God is at work even in those things which sometimes seem impossible. For you see, as long as I pray, I am at least receptive toward God, not rebelling against him or ignoring him. When I have that kind of attitude, I can be sure that he's at work.

I recall one night in my ministry that a call came to our house. It was the voice of a young man on the phone. Never had I heard the voice before. He told me that he was very distressed. He began to describe many of the perplexities of his life. He didn't give me a lot of details, however. He refused to give me his name. He wanted to remain anonymous and said that he was thinking of taking his life and wanted to know what my response to that would be; and what were some things he might need to think about with regard to that. I could have wished at that moment that I had taken crisis counseling, so that I could respond to the young man. He had told me so little, and I knew so little. I tried my best to answer, but I was greatly troubled all night because I feared that I had not answered him adequately. The next morning as I went to my study, my prayer was, "Lord, take what I did, use it for your glory; and if it is within your purpose, put that young man in touch with me again, so that I can do a better job, by your grace." Within thirty minutes of the time I had prayed, the phone rang. It was the young man. He was willing to give me his name. He was willing to come. We had opportunity to talk face to face. I had opportunity to minister to him in the name of the Lord. Our prayers are not always answered in that way, but I use that experience from my life to underscore the fact that God opens locked doors in response to prayer. I faced what appeared to be an impossible situation because there was no way I could have known who he was; no way I could have been in touch; no way I could have followed up. But I asked the Lord within his planned purpose to unlock that door; and in that case he did it in the way I described.

In conclusion, let me just say to us, I advocate prayer strongly in our lives, not because our praying gives God some kind of permission to do something. Not because we coerce God, for he will not be coerced. I don't advocate prayer because somehow God is going to move in the life of someone else and manipulate him in order that my prayers will be answered. But I am saying to us this morning that in God's economy of things, when a trusting child of his comes before him as Heavenly Father, we are more receptive, and somehow he sets in motion forces that are going to bring to pass in our lives that which is for our good and for his glory. We must, however, remain open to him. Refusing to pray is like having all the electrical power in the world available and refusing to plug in the appliance. When I as a child of his, refuse to converse in prayer, I am refusing to be in touch with him who has all power and who loves me so much. By my refusal, I deprive myself of the opportunity to see life from his perspective, to let him nurture his life in me, and to allow him to be at work in circumstances of my life in ways that he wants as my Lord.

"Our Father, we are grateful to you that you desire that we converse with you. We are grateful that you have made it possible for us to do so through Jesus Christ and that in the Word you have encouraged us to address you as our Father. We thank you for the intimate turf on which we can live with thee because we have been saved by your grace. We thank you that now that our great High Priest has made it possible for us to come with great boldness and with great confidence that you will give us grace and help. So as we move from this place, as we go about the responsibilities of this day, help us, O Lord, to be in touch with thee so that you might do in us your work so that we might be of more use to thee in our work. In the name of Christ, we pray. Amen."

NOTES

[1]Mark Twain, *The Adventures of Huckleberry Finn* (New York: Grosset and Dunlap Publishers, 1948), pp. 14–15.

[2]Winston Pearce, *Window Sill of Heaven* (Nashville: Broadman Press), p. 11.

[3]Charles Allen, *All Things Are Possible Through Prayer* (Westwood, New Jersey: Fleming H. Revell), preface.

Ferris Jordan, Professor of Adult Education and Chairman of the Division of Religious Education Ministries, has taught at New Orleans Baptist Theological Seminary since 1978. Prior to this he served twenty years in pastorates in Louisiana, Indiana, Illinois, and Tennessee. A graduate of Louisiana College (B.A.) and New Orleans Baptist Seminary (B.D. and Th.D.), he has written *Bible Teaching for Adults Through the Sunday School* and *Living Values for Today's Singles*. Jordan has also been a major contributor to *Adult Sunday School Work* and to *A Church Ministering to Adults*.

Believing in the Church

FISHER HUMPHREYS

Isaiah 57:14–15
1 Peter 2:9–10

If you ask Christian people what they believe in, the answer is a very clear one. We all have to say the same thing. We believe in God. Our religious faith has to be in the Lord himself. We believe that there is one and only one true and living God. We believe that he is the transcendent creator of this world, that he is eternally Father, and Son, and Spirit. We believe that the Father sent his Son into the world and he became one of us, Jesus of Nazareth. We believe that he gave his life upon the cross and rose again on the third day to save us from our sins. And we believe that the Father and the Son have poured their Spirit into our hearts whereby we have become the people of God, sent out on a world mission guided and empowered by the Spirit. When you ask Christians what they believe in, they have to say, "We believe in God."

We also believe that God is doing many important things in our world. We could talk about how sinners are being converted. We could talk about the Bible as the Word of God. We could talk about God stirring the hearts of people. There are many things that God is doing in this world, and we believe in them because we believe in God.

The one I want to talk to you about is believing in the church. We believe that the church is the people of God. We believe that God lives in a high and holy place. But we also believe that he lives among people of a humble and repentant heart. We believe that God has committed himself to be our God and called us to be his people. I believe in the church. I think the church is the chosen race. I think Christians are the priests of the King. I think the church is a holy nation. I think the church is God's own people. I believe in the church because I believe in the God who created the church.

When we talk about believing in the church, we do something interesting in our minds. I've noticed this over the years. When we say, I believe in the church, our minds go back to the early church, to the church of Acts and the Epistles. We naturally think the tremendous adventures of that church. We think about the way in which the Spirit of God worked with them, and they set out on a world mission that looked impossible, humanly speaking, but they managed to do it, to preach the gospel of Christ in Jerusalem and in Judea and unto the uttermost parts of the earth. We remember about how fresh and how bright the gospel was in the minds and hearts of people at that time, and we say, I believe in the church—back there. What a mission! What a people!

You know what we're doing when we do that, don't you? What we're doing is romanticizing the church. We're remembering the bright side and forgetting the shadows. We're remembering the good side and forgetting that there was another side to the life even of that church. We're forgetting their quarrels. We're forgetting that some of them were dishonest. We're forgetting the kinds of problems that they had in the church at Corinth. There is a dark side, even to that early church.

And yet, I believe in that church. I believe that church was the people of God. I believe that that church was the bride of Christ for whom Christ died. I believe that God loved that church, warts and all. And I believe that the church is always the people of God.

Sometimes when we talk about believing in the church we think about the church as it became worldwide, or at least empire-wide. We think about that victorious and illustrious church in which Emperors of Rome bowed their knees and their people followed their example. We think about the church of the creeds and the councils, the church that gave us the canon of Scripture and that gave us orthodoxy, the church of Athanasius and the church of Augustine, and we say, I believe in that church.

But again we're romanticizing. We're forgetting how often those Emperors used coercion to make the people bow their knees. We're forgetting the quarrels and the meanspiritedness of some of those great fathers of the church.

And yet, I believe in that church. I believe that church was the people of God, warts and all. I believe that church was the bride of Jesus Christ.

When we Baptists say, I believe in the church, our minds are likely to turn back to the time of Reformation. We're saying, in effect, I believe of the church of Luther and of Calvin. I believe with Luther that the church must be always being reformed, and that the only way the church can be reformed is to submit itself to the standard of Holy Scripture, not to traditions, not to the Magisterium of the church, but to Holy Scripture as the Word of God. We submit to that, and we allow the church to be reformed. When we study that Holy Scripture we learn that a human being can never justify himself in God's sight, but must always recognize that he has been justified by God's grace through his faith in Jesus Christ apart from the deeds of the law. And, because we are all justified by God's grace, we are all priests before God. We all have equal standing before our Lord and Savior Jesus Christ. So we say, I believe in that church, the church of the great Reformation.

And yet, once again, we're romanticizing the church. Have we forgotten that Luther wrote a book to the princes of Germany calling on them to use coercion against what he called swarming hoards of people who were carrying on their religion in ways that he thought were inappropriate? Have we forgotten that in Calvin's Geneva Servetus was burned at the stake because his theology was not orthodox? That church had its warts. It had its shadow side.

And yet, I believe in that church. I believe in the church of the Reformation, warts and all. I believe that it was the people of God. I believe that it was the bride of Christ, and that it is a wonderful and precious thing to be heirs of that great church.

With our Baptist heritage perhaps we think about believing in the church of the radical Reformation and of English separatist Puritianism. We think about that church made up of little tiny groups who were never an established religion. They were small and powerless and often persecuted because of their faith. They were people who made the case for peace and the case for justice and the case for freedom. They were a very humble people and didn't advertise themselves very much, but they were a stubborn people and they stood by their conviction that they were practicing their faith as God wanted them to do it. This was the church that eventually gave us Smythe and Helwys, that gave us Carey and Bunyan, and in this country gave us Roger Williams and John Leland. And we say, I believe in that church.

And yet, that too is a romanticizing. That church had its dark side as well, its narrowness, its refusal to accept the brotherhood of all Christian people. Sometimes it made mistakes, and I think they would have been the first to tell us that they made mistakes.

And yet, I believe in that church. I believe in those tiny little groups scattered around Europe and America, hounded by the powers, even by the churchly powers. I believe that church was the bride of Jesus, for whom Jesus died, and that he loved that church, and that God lived in the hearts of those people. I believe in that church, warts and all.

So we come today, to the churches that you and I know, that we experience, where we spend most of our lives. Small Baptist churches, middle-sized Baptist churches, perhaps sometimes, large Southern Baptist churches. We know what these churches are like, don't we? It's in our blood. We feel it. We know about their history. We know about their programs and their organizations. We know about the achievements of these churches. We know about their commitment to missions. We know about their commitment to evangelism. And we know about the growth that God has given us and blessed us with over these years. And we say, I believe in this church.

And yet, that can be a romanticizing, too. This church is a divided church. This church is a quarreling church. This church has sometimes been slow to change in ways that God wanted us to change. This church has sometimes been very narrow in the way in which it accepted other people, and insensitive to the needs of various people. This is a church also that has its shadow side.

And yet, I believe in this church. I believe in what is happening in Southern Baptist life. I believe that this is the people of God. I believe that this is the bride of Christ, whom Christ loves and for whom Christ died. I believe in this church. We need to believe in it without romanticizing. We need to believe in it, even when we know about the shadow side, when we know about the warts. I believe in this church as the people of God.

Now you might say to me, "Dr. Humphreys, you sound like a very gullible person. You're believing in an a lot of churches with all of those problems. Why do you do that? What's there to believe in? How can you have faith that God is really here among these people?" Those are serious questions. How can we believe in the church today? So many times I think that when we try to answer these questions, we begin by pointing out the good side of the church and the success of the church. But that's not what we ought to do. I believe in this church because I believe in the God of this church. I believe the church is bound in a covenant relationship with God. I believe that he has called us to be his people. And I believe God has committed himself to be the God of this people.

What is there to believe in in this church? There are many things I could talk about. One thing that I very much believe in is that this church is the family that keeps alive the memory of the crucified and risen Jesus. We believe the gospel that Christ died for our sins according to the Scriptures, and that he was buried, and that he rose to life again on the third day, according to the Scriptures. We preach this gospel. We teach this gospel. We sing this gospel. We celebrate this gospel. We dramatize this gospel by baptizing people and by celebrating the Lord's Supper. We remember the good news that Christ lived and died for our sins and rose again on the third day. I believe in this church because it is a gospel-centered church. It is centered upon the Lord Jesus Christ.

I read a little story by William Willimon, the Methodist minister. When his son was about six years old, he said to his father, "Daddy, I don't want to go to church." His father said, "Why not, son?" And the little boy said, "Because church is so boring." And Mr. Willimon said, "What's boring about the church?" And the little boy said, "It's just Jesus, Jesus, Jesus, that's all they ever talk about down at that church." Well, the church ought to be boring. We ought to talk about Jesus. That's one reason I believe in the church, because the church remembers the crucified and risen Jesus.

There's another reason I believe in the church. That is because the church is a place where people gather together to worship the Lord. We pray together. We sing songs such as the ones we have sung this morning. And we try to turn our hearts away from ourselves and turn toward God. The world teaches us to be concerned about ourselves, about our history and our money and our health and our friends and all the rest of it; but once a week we gather together and try for a few minutes to be concerned, not just about ourselves, but about the Lord. We try to worship God. We draw near to him. We turn our eyes upon Jesus.

That's why I believe in the church, because it is in fact a worshiping community. God does live in a high and holy place, but, my friends, he lives with people who are of a humble and repentant heart. God is here, and he draws us into the worship of himself. St. Augustine said that our hearts are restless until they find their rest in God, and I think it is true. So we gather together each week. Of course, lots of things change. The forms of worship change. But worship itself remains the same. We gather together each week, and, contrary to what the world teaches us, we try in fact to look toward God and to offer him our thanks and our worship. That's why I believe in the church.

I believe in the church for another reason as well. I believe in the church because the church is a group of people who are trying to be a family, who are learning to be friends with one another. We know that God has loved us, so we are trying to learn to love one another. The world doesn't teach us this. The world teaches us how to compete. The world teaches us how to be competent, how to get ahead, how to look out for number one, how to win through intimidation. That's what the world teaches us. But the church teaches us to be brothers and sisters together. It teaches us to live in the fellowship.

Out in the world I'm a customer. Out in the world I'm a patient or a client. But in the church I'm a brother. In the church we're all brothers and sisters together. We're learning together to live in a common life—the fellowship of the Holy Spirit. I believe in the church. I believe that in Sunday School and Church Training and prayer meetings, in revivals and church dinners and all the rest of it, we are gradually becoming a fellowship together, learning to respect one another, to love one another, to bear one another's burdens, and to pray for one another. That's why I believe in the church. God is doing this for us. He is drawing us together.

I hope you believe in the church too. You already know it, but I'll just tell you again. There are many things that will make you not believe in the church. There are many shadows. There are many warts. There are many things that will make you lose your faith in it. Many people have done it over the years. They have just said, I give up on the church.

But I hope you won't. God dwells in a high and holy place. But he does dwell with those who are of a humble and repentant heart. There is a family of God here on this earth. This family of God does remember the gospel of Jesus Christ. It does worship God, and it is gradually, at least, becoming a fellowship of the Holy Spirit. God lives in a high and holy place, but he also lives in the midst of these people.

"The church's one foundation is Jesus Christ Lord/She is his new creation by Spirit and the Word/From heaven he came and sought her to be his holy bride/With his own blood he bought her, and for her life he died."

Fisher Humphreys is Professor of Theology at New Orleans Baptist Theological Seminary. He holds degrees from Mississippi College, Loyola University, Oxford University, and New Orleans Baptist Theological Seminary, and he is the author of several books.

Priesthood of the Believer

J. TERRY YOUNG

1 Peter 2:9–10

Martin Luther was a troubled Roman Catholic monk. He found himself locked into a rigid authoritarian system, with a great deal imposed upon him through the structures of his church. At the same time, he attempted to be a responsible student of the Word; and, as he read its pages, a quiet storm began to develop within him. It finally welled up into gigantic proportions and he could be silent no longer. He tacked to the Wittenberg church door a list of 95 theses, or propositions, he felt needed to be examined in public discussion in the light of the Word of God. In so doing, he set off the Protestant Reformation, a revolution that had worldwide repercussions.

Somewhere in the mid 1940s, a man by the name of Hugh Fogle was a Sunday School teacher in the First Baptist Church at Houston. It was nearing promotion time. He took his Sunday School teaching very seriously. He came by the church office and asked if he might see the attendance record of the boys who were going to be promoted into his class on the first Sunday of October. Patiently he thumbed through the cards, one by one, noting who were faithful attenders; who were not; who were professed Christians, who were not. He systematically began pursuing his task of building a Sunday School class.

My name was on one of those cards, one of those blank cards. I had not been to Sunday School in that church for quite some time. It was my home church. But for several years in the early 40s, because of World War II, we were not able to travel the long distance from where we lived to church, and as a substitute had been attending a nearby neighborhood church spasmodically. I was at that critical teenage point where there was a fork in the road, where I was just discovering what was going on in life and wondering which direction to take. To my utter surprise, Hugh Fogle, who lived all the way across the city of Houston, came to see me on Saturday morning. He introduced himself to me, gave me a Sunday School quarterly and said, "I'm going to be your new Sunday School teacher, as of tomorrow morning. I surely would like to have you in my class." He began to tell me about some of the things he was planning to do with the fellows in that class.

I was astounded—astounded that anybody would care enough about me to drive all the way across the city of Houston just to say, "Sure would like to see you in Sunday School." I had been living along for a long time on the excuse that it was too far from where we lived to ride the bus. But if Hugh Fogle cared that much, I decided maybe I could get up a half-hour earlier and catch the bus and ride downtown to Sunday School. Hugh Fogle's Sunday School class was a revolutionary turning point for me.

What do those two incidents have in common? Martin Luther's revolution—Hugh Fogle's revolution? What brings those two widely separated events together? It is our cherished Baptist doctrine, the priesthood of believers. Each in his own way was expressing his commitment to this principle: the priesthood of believers.

We as Baptists believe that this is a doctrine rooted in Scripture itself. Indeed, if you look at 1 Peter 2:9, Peter employs that very term, priesthood, for every one of us as a believer. "But you are a chosen people, royal priesthood, a holy nation, a people belonging to God, that you may declare the praises of him who called you out of darkness into his wonderful light."

Now I could cite for you other passages of Scripture employing that same terminology and others which use the priestly idea, though not the term. But I want to suggest to you that this idea of the priesthood of believers is more basic than one or two or merely a sampling of Scriptures. It's a thread that runs all the way through the Bible from first to last; or perhaps better, it is like the canvas on which is painted the entirety of the biblical message.

You cannot separate this idea of the priesthood of believers from basic biblical Christianity; not without doing violence to what the Scriptures teach. The priesthood of believers had been a long forgotten doctrine in Martin Luther's day. Luther rediscovered it, emphasized it, brought it back to the consciousness of millions of people. We as Baptists picked up on it and began to magnify it. It has been part and parcel of our preaching for all the centuries of our existence.

And yet I discover in our churches it is one of the least understood doctrines we have. Indeed it is one of those cherished possessions we could lose in our generation if certain people are allowed to prevail. I want you to think for a few minutes about this idea of priesthood of believers. And I hope you notice that I am speaking in the plural—priesthood of believers. I like that emphasis. I'm borrowing it from Walter B. Shurden who wrote the doctrine study book (*The Doctrine of the Priesthood of Believers*, Convention Press, 1987) being used in many of our churches this spring. Not the priesthood of the believer, but the priesthood of believers. It is not just a private right I enjoy, but it is a communal experience in which all of us as Christians share. Very often we magnify one aspect or another of this priesthood theme at the expense of the whole truth.

I want to suggest to you there are two sides of the coin when we talk of the priesthood of believers. And the truth is not in either phase, but in holding those two phases in a working tension or polarity. Just as with the battery in your automobile, there is a negative and a positive terminal and neither is worth anything apart from relationship to the other. And so with this theme, the priesthood of believers.

I would suggest to you that actually there are three sets of polarities that need to be understood when we talk about priesthood of believers. One of those sets is privilege and responsibility. Very often we are quick to emphasize the privilege of priesthood, stressing the fact that I as an individual have the right of free access to God for my salvation, for my prayer life, for my study of the Scriptures. But along with that privilege there is also responsibility: responsibility to take my salvation very seriously; responsibility for carrying out the Great Commission. The privelege of priesthood includes the responsibility to exercise the opportunity for interpretation of the Scriptures. Feeding my heart from the truths of God's Word, not taking second hand what you pass on to me. Feeding my own soul at the banquet table of God's Word; the responsibility to maintain my own prayer life. While I do solicit your prayers on my behalf, your prayers for me are no substitute for my own prayer life. The privilege that I have in addressing God in prayer demands that I exercise that privilege freely, regularly, responsibly.

The responsibility attached to this priesthood of believers also requires that I respect your privilege as a priest under God. I must allow you the same privilege of settling your soul's relationship with God that I claim for myself. I must grant to you the same privilege to open Scripture and search its pages for the word of God speaking to you that I expect for myself. And though you may not always interpret Scripture as I interpret it, I must respect you with the same respect that I want you to have for me.

At the moment that any one of us tries to impose his own view upon another, compromising that individual's priesthood, at that moment he has ceased to be a priest and has started to play God instead. No one of us should dare to try to play the role of God. The priesthood of believers means that I may help you in your search for God. Indeed I may do my best to try and point you to God when you're not even looking for him. But in no way can I stand between you and God. I cannot prevent your crying out to God for salvation, nor can I give you the gift of salvation. That's priestly hocus pocus and not priesthood of believers. Priesthood of believers involves, on the one hand, privilege; on the other hand, responsibility.

But I want to point out a second pair of polarities here. There is, on the one hand, an individual aspect of this priesthood, and over against that individual aspect there is the community aspect. I as an individual am a priest of the most high God. I have the right of direct access to him; I also have the responsibility to be his ambassador to all this world. But at the same time, the New Testament knows nothing of a "lone ranger" Christianity, each of us riding off into the sunset in isolation from all the rest.

Everywhere in the New Testament that I find believers it is always in the context of a fellowship of believers, a community of believers, the body of the Lord Jesus Christ, the church of the living God. The priesthood of believers is not a license for unbridled individualism, though I hear some folk talk about the priesthood of believers as though they have some kind of license from almighty God to do their own thing in contradiction to what all the rest of the world may be doing. While I have the tremendous personal advantage of direct approach to God for myself, I must always remember that God has saved me, not that I might be one lone isolated voice on the horizon, but that I might take my place in responsible life and activity in the church, the body of Christ. And in that body of Christ finding what my particular role is.

As Paul developed the theme of the body of Christ, he took great pains in several passages of Scripture to point out that while we are all members of the body of Christ, there is an amazing diversity of members. Not all can be an eye. Not all can be a mouth. Not all can be a hand. We need to recognize that diversity, and respect that diversity. Indeed, we should cultivate that diversity. The body functions well only when all its various parts are in good working order. What a strange body it would be, as Paul suggests, if every member were to suddenly exclaim, "Oh, I can have nothing to do with these other parts. I'm a hand. I want to work with, I want to associate with, I want to fellowship only with those who are a hand just like me. Not any hand, not a left hand, only a right hand."

Priesthood of believers means that not only do we have the personal blessings of God, but we are intimately caught up in what God is doing in the church, building a community of faith of diverse people--young and old, short and tall, fat and skinny, learned and ignorant, rich and poor, black and white, and on and on. We must not take alarm at that diversity, or try to squelch that diversity, but encourage and promote and develop that diversity. Respect it. Which means that I have to give you the freedom to be what God made you to be, hoping and praying that by like turn, you will accord me that same freedom under God. Individuality and community—either without the other is a distortion of the truth.

There is a third set of polarities here. That's the investment of your own dedicated efforts in service to God on the one hand, and the Spirit of God equipping you and working through you on the other hand. I cannot sit back and merely fold my arms and say, "Lord you called me, and if you want to use me, start pouring it out through me." A young friend of mine came to the pulpit one Sunday morning and announced to the congregation where he was the invited guest speaker for the day, "I am yielded to God and I am willing to do whatever he wants me to do. I asked him if he had a message for me to give you today. Since he didn't give me one, we'll have the dismissal prayer." And he's been wondering ever since then why they didn't invite him back to speak again.

God promises to bless and guide and use and work through us, but nowhere does he promise to do it for us. I think priesthood of believers requires that we pour into everything we do the best dedicated efforts we can muster; working, praying, preaching as though everything depended on our own individual work. But at the same time, resting in the firm faith that God will bless and work through every effort we put forth for him. He will give us gifts. He will pour his power into us. But only when we're willing to meet him half way and put forth our best efforts.

Priesthood of believers is a rich and meaningful doctrine underlying the entirety of our Christian faith and practice. Don't sell it short. Don't let someone take it from you. It's easier to preserve than to win again once it's lost.

J. Terry Young is Professor of Theology at New Orleans Baptist Theological Seminary. He came to the faculty in 1971 from California, where he had been editor of The California Southern Baptist, 1963–1971. Prior to that he served as pastor in California and Texas. He was born in Houston, TX. He earned the B.A. degree from Baylor, the B.D. and Th.D. at Southwestern Baptist Theological Seminary. He is the author of three books: *The Church—Alive and Growing*, *The Spirit within You*, and *Compelled by the Cross*. He also contributed to *The Birth of Churches* and the *Disciple's Study Bible*.

The Pursuit Of Peace

CLAUDE L. HOWE, JR.

For the kingdom of God is not eating and drinking, but justice, peace, and joy, inspired by the Holy Spirit. He who thus shows himself a servant of Christ is acceptable to God and approved by men. Let us then pursue the things that make for peace and build up the common life. Rom. 14:17–19, (NEB).

Christians differ about many things. They always have and they always will. Some have died for making the sign of the cross with two fingers rather than three. Fellowship has been broken over whether one should wash both feet or only one—footwashing or feetwashing. Here they differ about food and days, with the vegetarians against the meat-eaters and those who would observe special days against those who would not.

For many these matters are incidental, but for others essential. Christians agree readily that there are essentials and non-essentials, but precisely identifying and defining them is another task. What is relatively unimportant for one may be absolutely necessary for the other.

Differences produce judgment, not only of issues but of persons. The strong are over against the weak, the conservatives are opposed to the moderates, the true believer against the apostate. Some conform to one side or the other without being fully convinced and so violate conscience. In this broad context Paul advises Christians to pursue the things that make for peace and mutual upbuilding.

Southern Baptist Christians differ about many things. They always have and they always will. Some have been open and others closed communionists. Some have been pre and others post or amillennialists. Now they differ not about food and days but about words and ways—words about the Bible and ways of cooperating.

The patterns already described continue to operate—incidental or essential, issues or persons, judge and despise, conform or rebel. No doubt the suggestions of Paul are applicable here also. He did not say appoint a committee, which is what Baptists usually do, though he would not object to this as a beginning.

But he did say, "Let us then pursue the things that make for peace and build up the common life." The focus at this point was not upon world peace or individual peace, as important as these may be, but upon peace in the Christian community. Note the larger reality, the needed reminder, and the specific request of the apostle.

I. THE LARGER REALITY

"The kingdom of God is not eating and drinking, but justice, peace, and joy, inspired by the Holy Spirit." Christians easily become enamored with the moment or the movement at hand and lose perception of the larger reality. Paul calls upon these Christians to develop a perspective encompassing the kingdom of God.

Dr. Hardee Kennedy occasionally reminded students at New Orleans Seminary of truth contained in a nursery rhyme. "Pussy can, pussy cat, where have you been? I've been to London to see the Queen. Pussy cat, pussy cat, what did you there? I chased a mouse under the chair." Imagine the scene: "I was in the Imperial Palace in the presence of the King! What did you there? I chased a liberal or a fundamentalist under a chair."

Paul encourages us to evaluate the moment or the movement in the context of the kingdom or kingly rule of God. Both zeal and despair are tempered, for victory does not depend entirely on us nor is it assured for others. God rules, and when God rules, priorities shift from the material to the spiritual, from the temporal to the eternal. If justice becomes manipulation, if peace becomes turmoil, if joy becomes bitterness, these are not inspired by the Holy Spirit. When God rules, justice and peace and joy in the Holy Spirit prevail.

The task of the Christian is clear. Seek first the kingdom of God. Pray thy kingdom come, thy will be done. When God rules, humans are freed to serve, not forced to judge. Freedom may be used rightly to extend the kingdom of God, not to build the kingdoms of men.

II. THE NEEDED REMINDER

"He who thus shows himself a servant of Christ is acceptable to God and approved by men." With these words Paul points back to the entire discussion of food and days, reminding Christians that Christ is Lord, that Christians are servants, that love is paramount.

Christ is Lord. He died and came to life again to establish his lordship over dead and living. The proper response to him is one of worship and trust. Christians are responsible and accountable to Christ alone. Those who would predict anarchy can trust the Lord. Each of us will answer to Christ for himself.

Christians are servants. The servant of Christ does not judge or condemn or hinder one for whom Christ died. Accept the brother without attempting to settle all doubtful points. Whether the brother stands or falls is the business of the Master, not the fellow servant. The power of the Master will enable him to stand.

Love is paramount. Freedom in Christ is guided by love for the brother. Freedom gives choice. One may refrain even from that which is regarded as a right because of concern or love for the brother. Such servants are acceptable to God and approved by men.

III. THE SPECIFIC REQUEST

"Let us then pursue the things that make for peace and build up the common life." Pursuit of peace is very important for every Christian, but this pursuit indicates a direction, not a position. Paul speaks to the strong and to the weak, to the moderate and to the conservative, and says pursue the things that make for peace. One may start from a particular position and the brother from another but the closer they get to peace the closer they are together. Not one side or the other side but all sides are to pursue the things that make for peace.

Pursuit of peace stresses acceptance more than agreement. The place to begin is not by settling doubtful points but by accepting persons whom God has accepted. In doing that, agreement may or may not come but it is God who guides the process. Trust him to do so rightly. Pursuit of peace stresses acceptance more than agreement.

Pursuit of peace highlights responsibilities more than rights. We live in a time when various kinds of rights are being asserted strongly, and surely there is a time to exercise rights. But there is a greater time to exercise responsibility, so in pursuit of our rights we try to be responsible to God and to the brother.

Pursuit of peace seeks unity more than uniformity. Not every person must eat the same thing. If one is a vegetarian and another a meat-eater, the kingdom of God does not collapse. If one holds up one day over another, the same is true. Unity of spirit and heart and mind and goal are more significant than uniformity in every belief and practice for the kingdom of God.

Pursuit of peace supports the constructive rather than the destructive, that which builds up rather than that which tears down. Pursue the things that build up the common life. Mutual upbuilding requires patient endeavor and active support while mutual destruction requires only benign neglect or selfish promotion.

Pursuit of peace respects conviction but remembers conscience. Both are important. Christian belief is important.

Do not let anyone presume that it is not. Christian behavior is important. Let none convince you otherwise. Christian fellowship is important and will remain so. In each of these pursue the things that make for peace and build up the common life. In verse twenty-two, Paul sort of wraps it up. "If you have a clear conviction, apply it to yourself in the sight of God." Apply it to yourself, to yourself. "Happy is the man who can make his decision with a clear conscience." So, the word for each of us today is pursue the things that make for peace and build up the common life.

Dr. Howe is a native of Senatobia, Mississippi, and a graduate of Mississippi College, Purdue University, and the New Orleans Seminary. He has taught Church History at the Seminary for three decades and also serves as Chairman of the Theological and Historical Studies Division.

The Smell of Sulfur—The Clerical Syndrome

MACKLYN W. HUBBELL

Dean Cothen, this portends to be my greatest hour. As I stand here in this sanctuary with the seating capacity of something like 2000, I see only a few hundred people. This could be my grandest hour. In speaking the way I've just spoken, the last sentence or two reminds me of two personalities who are important "traditions" associated with our institution. One involves Dr. Hardee Kennedy. I had never met Dr. Kennedy. In 1980, in December, when I came to New Orleans International Airport, this distinguished gentleman met me at the gate and introduced himself, "I'm Hardee Kennedy." I said "I'm Macklyn Hubbell." We talked lightly for a few moments. Then he said, "How was your trip?" And I said, "Fine trip, Dr. Kennedy." Then I remarked, "I'll tell you what. I'll go and get my luggage and meet you at the end of the corridor." He said, "Dr. Hubbell, may I make a counter-proposal?" "Well," I thought to myself, "I don't know whether I want you to do that or not—before God and everybody, right here with so many people around." I had no earthly idea what was coming next. I said, "Why, of course, Dean, you can make a counter-proposal!" "May I go and get your luggage? You stand here and I will meet you in a few moments with your luggage?" I was so relieved to know what a counter-proposal was and to know what counter-proposal he had made. "Why, yes, Dean, go right ahead. Get my luggage and meet me here in a few minutes."

There's another person who is a "tradition"—a very important person. What I'm going to say now is relevant to what I'm going to say in a few minutes. This "tradition" is named Martha Haney. Now, we have computers in our registry office. We did not need computers as long as Martha Haney was around. She remembered all the little things and she remembered all the big things. In a New York second she could retrieve anything at any time. I spoke on the subject that I'm speaking on today. I would like to say that after I spoke on this subject to the Profettes, many people came to me and said, "Mack, you need to speak this again and again!" But only Martha Haney came and said, "You must speak this in chapel." I said, "Martha Haney, I haven't spoken in chapel in a long time, but if I ever get a chance I'll use this same material." And so, Martha Haney, the one who remembers everything, may word get to you in one way or another that I am fulfilling my obligation to you and my promise to you. Today, I repeat that presentation entitled "The Smell of Sulfur" or subtitled, "The Clerical Syndrome."

A few years ago, my wife and I were living in a little place called Wallis, Texas. I say a little place: I'm talking about a real little place—a drug store, a filling station, and a First Baptist church of Wallis—that's about all. In order to allow us to go to Europe, which we'd planned to do in a matter of a year or so, I, in addition to working at the church as pastor of the church, worked in a sulfur field called Duval Sulfur. Every morning I would get up early. My wife would pack my lunch. I would head toward the little blue bus that would take me through Orchard to Duval Sulfur where I was classified as a member of the "bull gang." If you don't know what a "bull gang" is, I can't describe it other than saying that everything, anything, no one else wanted to do, that's what we did. In the process of working on this "bull gang" for Duval Sulfur Company, I was exposed to big mounds of sulfur. When I came home at night, I smelled life sulfur. I rubbed Dial soap over all the cutaneous parts of me. I tried to get rid of that smell of sulfur. I took Aqua-Velva shaving lotion and rubbed it all over my face expecting my wife to say, "Honey, you smell just right." Instead she would always say, "Honey, you still smell like sulfur." Now if my children had been born at this time, they would have said in no uncertain terms—"Daddy, you stink!" Do you know, it took weeks and maybe even months to wear off this smell of sulfur. Now the upshot is this: you and I as clerics tend to bring home the smell of our profession with us. We work around Greek lexicons. We work around Thomas Helwys. We work around John Calvin. We work around great ideas and great persons. When we go home, we tend to smell like our profession. Or we work in our church offices, and surround ourselves with holy things. When we come home, we tend to smell like "sulfur."

We take these undesirable parts of our professions or vocations and make these a part of us. They become a part of us. They become a part of our persons.

May I suggest that you and I may be victims of the *Tylenol Syndrome*? About two or three years ago, there was a scare in Chicago which tended to permeate the whole United States. It went everywhere. You and I were frightened here as well. At least I was frightened. I didn't take Tylenol, but I wouldn't even walk close to where Tylenol was stocked. I was afraid of Tylenol. Then I got afraid of milk. Maybe someone has laced the milk with cyanide. I was afraid of anything that was packaged. Well, you know what I'm talking about when I refer to Bob Green's article in the Times-Picayune on October 9, 1982:

> I hear people saying: "I almost took a Tylenol this morning, but I took an aspirin instead." And, "I was just going to the store to buy some Tylenol." They were acting as if the story really had everything to do with the product called Tylenol. It doesn't. It has to do with the idea that living today is an act of faith. Every time you order a meal in a restaurant, you have faith that someone in the kitchen didn't put something deadly in your food. Every time you open up a bottle of soda pop, you have faith that someone at the factory didn't decide that a drinker should die. Every time you buy

any kind of medicine over the counter, you have faith that what you swallow is what the label says you are going to swallow. If you think about everything that could go wrong during your day, it will make you crazy.

Somehow or another you and I take on certain characteristics and bring these characteristics home. One of the characteristics is the Tylenol syndrome. We become suspicious of people, somewhat paranoid. As students (as I look out here, and see this great congregation of students), I realize that sometimes you become very suspicious of us as faculty members. You ask: "What are their motives? What are they going to do to us next?" You see the syllabi, wondering how in the world can you achieve all of this? You become very suspicious of us. You may even become suspicious of other people, your colleagues and your fellow students. We may become quite suspicious as faculty members. We may become suspicious of recorders in classes. We become even suspicious of the administration or each other. The administration may become suspicious of students and their motives. They may become suspicious of what's going on in the Dodd Building—very suspicious, very paranoid. And as pastors we may become suspicious of people that we work with. Who are these deacons? What are they going to do to us? We become suspicious of fellow staff members. You know, that music director—what's he trying to do to me? What's the choir trying to do? Is this a lobbying group?

To live in distrust is to live miserably. I am not suggesting reckless abandon nor am I suggesting naivete. I am suggesting a simple trust in God and acceptance of people as people.

Then, there is the *Black Suit Syndrome*. There is a tradition among us that the minister should wear black. I don't know where this came from. Maybe it came from Hollywood or the Roman priesthood. I don't know where it cam from, but it's very typical of the minister playing a role. He wears black, because he is expected to wear black. This may not be so different from the nurse who wears white or the businessman in Washington, D.C. or Philadelphia or New York City who wears the grey or dark blue suit. It's not so different from the teenager. The teenage female may tie herself up in a fadish outfit. However, this syndrome suggests that there is a certain unalterable way of dressing no matter what our personalities call for. This can mean a number of things. On the one hand, it can mean inflexibility. I've got to do it this way or I've been told it's got to be done this way. Or it can mean to the cleric conforming to group patterns. It can mean the denial of personality expression. Of course, it can mean a person prefers black or just likes black.

Now there is a beautiful me under that black suit if I will allow me to come out from under that black suit. There is a me that God has created and that other people need to see. And there's a me that God has recreated that other people need to see.

There's the *Junior Chamber of Commerce Syndrome*. When I think of the Jaycees I think of these four words: busy, busy, busy, and busy. I see these people go around who call themselves Jaycees and they make me weary. They're so busy doing so much. They do participate in worthwhile activities I must admit. But often they don't take the time to see the blue of the sky or the red of the roses. They just don't take the time and the cleric is likewise very busy. The cleric does not think in terms of simple addition; he's got to think in terms of multiplication. He's busy with the church organization, busy "playing church," and even busy "being church." Granted, there is a pace that the cleric in his environment feels he must maintain, but even this could be reduced. The "business" has influenced enjoying the ordinary which often is the extraordinary, namely, being with our families, our wives, our children, and other meaningful persons.

Then, there is the *Sheltered Daughter Syndrome*. You know the sheltered daughter of the early 1900's. We even have a few sheltered daughters today among clerics. The cleric tends to be sheltered. When I served in Anderson, South Carolina, I remember a little ritual we went through every time I went to the barber shop. In those days, I went to the barber shop weekly. Any time a hair touched my ear, I had to go to the barber shop. This is the ritual I went through: Paul Teasley was in the first chair because he was of first importance, like the first violinist. He was important. He could do the best job in the whole shop. Every time I walked into the barber shop, Paul would say, "Hey, Preacher!" He wasn't just addressing me, instead he was announcing to the barber shop that there was a minister in the shop. "Clean up your acts" was the message. I also remember playing golf in Anderson. The green fees were posted. They had a green fee for men, for women, and for the clergy. I always wondered what was so different in me that I had got a green fee all by myself.

The cleric tends to live the sheltered life. He tends not to be exposed to the world outside. I'm not talking about contamination. I'm not talking about compromise. I'm talking about exposing oneself to the real world outside, people in life outside. I'm not necessarily talking about Bourbon Street, but I am talking about Bourbon Street. I'm talking about Ruby Red's restaurant—a place you take your life in your own hands to find. But you get there and you discover a part of life. I'm talking *Time* magazine. I'm talking about 42nd street, the Irish parade, and "The Gods Must be Crazy." I'm talking about exposing ourselves to the world. By not being exposed, we tend to know only about a specialized world of holiness. We tend to know only about what happens here at 3939 Gentilly, or know Beulah Baptist statistics or be familiar with the Sunday School picnic. We become boringly in-house!

There is also the *Seam Allowance Syndrome*. Those of you who sew may know what I'm talking about. Those of you who don't, I am referring to the seam that you can feel inside your garment. Now, the cleric talks so much about holiness for so many consecutive hours. He talks and continues to talk about sanctification, Thomas Helwys, the written Word or even God. But, when he comes home to his family, he tends to expose them only to that which is the underseam side of his life. He is sarcastic with his family.

He's abrupt with his family. He's abrasive with them or he is just plain rude. Yet, his family deserves his best. His family deserves his kindest words, his most thoughtful gestures and his best behavior.

And finally, there is the *Pharaoh Syndrome*. I recall the gist of the Moses-Pharaoh dialogue. One said, "Let my people go" and the other said, "I'll let them go," but deep down he said, "No, I ain't going to let them go." You recall how Pharaoh vacillated. He was back and forth, but basically he was saying, "No! I'm not going to let these people go!" The cleric tends to say to his own family members, "No, "I'm not going to let you go. I'm not going to release you. I was called and you are called." He has to live a certain way and he is going to have them to live a certain way. They reflect him. He is very important. When people see his family, they think of him. It is the "I" that he is really concerned about. He's not concerned about them. The end result is that he stifles the growth potential of his family. He will create resentment because they want freedom to choose. He is basically interfering with what God wants them to be. It is distasteful, to say the least, for any of us to choose the vocation for any of our family members. After all, God is still at work and God can bring about growth in our family members. The Holy Spirit is still at work and he can work in the lives of our family members. He's not limited and God is still at work. He can call people to do whatever he wants, including our family members.

What I have said about the cleric is true more or less of all people in their profession. Their lifestyles are often dictated or influenced by their profession. This is not altogether unhealthy. It is only unhealthy when it binds and restricts us from being what God wants us and our families to be and, in turn, what we ourselves want to be.

The saying is sure: If any one aspires to the office of bishop, he desires a noble task. Now a bishop must be above reproach, the husband of one wife, temperate, sensible, dignified, hospitable, and apt teacher, no drunkard, not violent but gentle, not quarrelsome, and

no lover of money. He must manage his own household well, keeping his children submissive and respect-
ful in every way; for if a man does not know how to
manage his own household, how can he care for God's
church? He must not be a recent convert, or he may be
puffed up with conceit and fall into the condemnation
of the devil; moreover, he must be well thought of by
outsiders, or he may fall into reproach and the snare of
the devil (1 Timothy 3:1–7).

For eighteen years prior to coming to the New Orleans
Baptist Theological Seminary in 1980 as Associate Professor
in Psychology and Counseling, Macklyn W. Hubbell served
as pastor of the First Baptist Church, Cleveland, Missis-
sippi. He received a B.A. degree from Baylor University, an
M.A. from University of Houston, a B.D. and Th.M. from
Southern Seminary, and a Ph.D. from the University of
Southern Mississippi. He is the author of *Being A Good
Senior Samaritan* and *Helping the Hurting*.

Musings Along LA-1 and I-10

LANDRUM P. LEAVELL II

2 Timothy 4:1–8

One of my favorite passages from the pen of Paul is found in the fourth chapter of 2 Timothy, verses 1–8:

> I charge thee therefore before God, and the Lord Jesus Christ, who shall judge the quick and the dead at his appearing and his kingdom; Preach the word; be instant in season, out of season; reprove, rebuke, exhort with all longsuffering and doctrine. For the time will come when they will not endure sound doctrine; but after their own lusts shall they heap to themselves teachers, having itching ears; And they shall turn away their ears from the truth, and shall be turned unto fables. But watch thou in all things, endure afflictions, do the work of an evangelist, [didn't say be a called evangelist in full-time service, but do the work of an evangelist] make full proof of thy ministry. For I am now ready to be offered, and the time of my departure is at hand. I have fought a good fight, I have finished my course, I have kept the faith: Henceforth there is laid up for me a crown of righteousness, which the Lord, the righteous judge, shall give me at that day, and not to me only, but unto all them also that love his appearing.

On Tuesday night of this week the Development Department here at the seminary sponsored a banquet in Shreveport, Louisiana. It was for the purpose of saying "thank you" to friends of New Orleans Seminary in Shreveport. Over one hundred people had gathered there.

In that meeting a man came up to me and said, "Landrum, what kind of folks are you trying to turn out down there at New Orleans Seminary?" Now for the benefit of those of you who might not be familiar with that vernacular, he was asking me, "What kind of graduates are you endeavoring to produce at New Orleans Seminary?" What kind of people are we trying to turn out down here in New Orleans?

It was against the background of that question that I spent considerable time yesterday, driving down the highway, seeking to come to grips with an answer. So, I've entitled what I'm going to say this morning, "Musings Along LA-1 and I-10."

If you've ever traveled LA-1, it's not one of the greatest highways in America. In fact, it may be one of the worst, and I don't recommend that you do what I did, that is, drive along LA-1 with a pencil in hand and a piece of paper jotting down a few notes. But I did exactly that, and I want to share that with you today.

There is a difference in seminary graduates. You know that as well as I. We might even be able to say that there are differences in the graduates of various seminaries. I don't think our Southern Baptist seminaries are turning out the same kind of graduates that Notre Dame Seminary here in our city is graduating. There is a difference. There's a difference in the ministry that graduates perform after they've finished the seminary. For instance, as I look around (and I do have some familiarity with the Southern Baptist convention and the churches of our convention), it seems to me that the scholars are on one side presiding over static or declining churches while those with minimal training, often with bogus "store-bought" degrees, are with single-minded commitment building strong churches and winning numbers of people to Christ. Have you observed that? That's a problem. It's a problem with which we grapple in theological education and particularly one with which I try to deal.

The question comes, is it possible for a highly trained and highly educated person to remain warm-hearted and evangelistic and be a church-builder? We've got to face that question, folks, because building churches and winning people to Christ is the future of who we are. If we don't do that, we don't have a future. There won't be a Southern Baptist Convention for other generations if we're not warm-hearted and evangelistic and involved in building strong witnesses for Christ.

Let me put it another way. This thought occurred to me in my musings along the swamps of LA-1. Can a person with an earned Th.D. degree grow a "super" church? The answer to which I came is "Yes!" It can be done, but you can name them in the Southern Baptist Convention on the fingers of one hand, and maybe have a finger or two left over. What's happening? What occurs in the rigors of graduate education that is accredited and high quality that somehow diverts us from what we ought to be and what we're here to do? Is it true, the accusation that we so often hear frequently made by those who don't know, "You don't need to go to seminary. . . . They'll ruin you down there?"

Unfortunately, I have seen some warm-hearted, evangelistic folks come to this campus and who have left here far different from the way they came as far as their evangelistic outreach and ministry is concerned.

The answer I gave to that man, who is a former mayor of Bossier City, Louisiana, was: "Jake, all we can do on campus is try to aim them." That is certainly something that needs to be done and we must know the direction in which students should be aimed.

Paul was talking about this sort of thing in the words of our text. I believe that's what it's all about. He is admonishing Timothy to follow in the role that he has patterned. Paul has already done it. He's saying to Timothy this is what I have done and I commend it to you.

I pray that we're going to graduate *prepared persons*.

Now, what I'm going to say today is alliterative, and I know that's not recommended in some quarters, but on the other hand, I want you to remember it, and that's the reason

I'm doing it. [You'll catch that after awhile.]

Prepared persons will have a number of characteristics. First of all, I pray that our graduates will be *people persons.* That's pretty simple. I'm just saying those who graduate should be people who love people. Some of you don't. I have observed it. Some of you appear to have inferiority complexes because you walk around the campus as though you had lost a dime and you're trying to find it. You don't look up, you don't speak to people, you just kind of "ooze" along. A people person is going to be interested in people, and if you're not interested in people, get a job somewhere out in the secular world and let some people-loving persons have the place that you might occupy and keep someone else from getting. People persons. I see people who walk by and who never speak; who ride up and down the streets and never look to the right or the left, never wave; they're not friendly, they're not interested in people. If you're interested in people, you're going to be involved in their lives. You're at least going to be friendly and speak when you see them.

New Orleans is not the friendliest place on earth. You can walk the streets of this city day or night and probably no one will ever speak to you unless it's another New Orleans Seminary student. That's contagious, you know, and we can help make this a friendly city.

I want to tell you a little experience that I've had. There's a man in a place of business downtown, a parking garage where I park regularly to attend a civic club meeting that I attend weekly in the downtown area. He was the coldest, most indifferent person you ever saw—wouldn't even grunt when he came up to hand me a ticket. I started jumping out of my car, waiting for him to walk up, and I'd say, "Hello there, neighbor." He'd look at me, and finally he got where he'd make a little unintelligible noise like, "Um huh huh." Yesterday—this hasn't taken but twelve years—when I pulled into the garage, he was there, waiting for me, and he walked half-way out to the street talking with me. I've learned a little bit about him. I know something about his family. I know what church he goes to. I know a whole lot about him now that I never would have learned if I had not continued to make the effort.

Be a people person. Love people enough to try to make friends with them. I hope every graduate of this institution will be that kind of person. A genuine love for people can be spotted instantaneously and sham can be discerned just as readily.

So, to my friend in north Louisiana, I would say, I hope we'll graduate *people persons.*

There's another characteristic. I pray we'll graduate *peaceable persons.* You know, if you become a peace-maker this is not merely a peace-keeper. You can be a pacifist and be a peace-keeper, but if you are a peace-maker, the chances are excellent that you will get bumped around a little bit and bruised in the process. I'm here to tell you today, up front, that the viability and the future usefulness of the Southern Baptist Convention is going to rest upon people who are peaceable, peace-making people.

Peace depends on every human being, under God, having a little bit of his own elbow room. If you try to put me in a straight-jacket and make me believe what somebody else believes, simply because they believe it, or make me say it the way they say it simply because that's the way it's been said by others, you're going to have trouble with me. I wasn't built that way! Your're going to have to give me a little room.

By the same token, if I expect you to give me a little space, I'm going to have to give you a little. There may have been injustices on one side or the other in the Southern Baptist Convention, but we're not going to solve the problem by doing the same thing to another group that the first group says was done to them. That's where we are, folks, and we may live to see the whole thing fragmented simply because there are not any peaceable people who are willing to live their own lives, under God, and let other people have that same privilege.

The thing that really concerns me is the number of younger preachers in our denomination today who are voting a party ticket. Brother, if you haven't got sense enough to make up your own mind and somebody else has to tell you how to vote, you might as well live in Russia. You might as well just pull on out and go over yonder and let them tell you how to do and when to do it. If you're a Christian, a Spirit-filled Christian, you don't have to have anyone tell you how to vote. You don't have to have anyone tell you what is best for you or for the Southern Baptist Convention. You can go to a convention and make up your own mind. You can be your own man, and I would pray God that the graduates of this institution will be that. I'm not telling you who to vote for, I'm telling you to vote for the one you feel God wants you to vote for, not someone you've been told to vote for.

What kind of graduates do we want to turn out—people persons, peaceable persons, then *positive persons.*

Have you ever noticed the number of people who have what we could call "buzzard religion?" Let me explain that to you. You've seen them, always soaring around, just looking for something dead and stinking. I hope you won't think I'm being crude, but I know that kind of person. Always looking for something negative and off-beat and always quick to repeat it to the widest possible audience. If you had to verify everything you say before you said it, we'd have a quiet world. Most conversation would cease. Be a positive person.

You know, when our song leader said a minute ago, "Share a blessing with somebody close to you," I wanted to stand up and say, "Thank you Lord for as beautiful a day as anybody ever witnessed." Thank God for a day like this, not a cloud in the sky, pleasant and cool, no wind, everything is super. Boy, it's just a great day to be alive. Be positive. You can always find something to be positive about.

Some of you don't know anything about prom parties. That's the sort of parties they used to have for us when we were kids—that is in my generation—Dr. Cothen's and mine. One little boy's mother told him, "Now, Son, when you go out on a prom with each of those little girls, say nice things about them. Say something nice about every little girl you promenade with." He was doing pretty well.

Everybody—all the little girls—had on a pretty flower or pretty dress, but finally one of the ones he had to promenade with was a little, short, fat girl who just didn't have much to commend her. When they got back from the prom, he had not said a word the whole time they were walking. When they got back to the party he looked at her and blurted out, "You sweat less than any little fat girl I ever saw." You can find something to be positive about.

Let me give you another characteristic. I would hope the ones who graduate from this institution will be *persistent persons*. I am referring to the kind of people who set their own agenda and follow it. Don't let somebody else write your agenda for you. If you work in a Baptist church there are lots of people who will write your agenda. You'll spend your time greasing the wheels that are squeaking, and you'll never seem to get anything done. You ought to know where you're going and how to get there. Every graduate of this institution, with whatever degree, ought to be a life-long-learner committed to a life-long growth process. That's the only kind of commitment which will prevent spiritual and intellectual stagnation in your life—a life-long-learner, a persistent person. Don't give up, just stay with it. "We'll reap in due season, if we faint not." That's the promise of The Book.

Let me add one other word or characteristic. I would hope that our graduates will be *pious persons*. I'm not saying "holier than thou;" that's the kind of person who turns us all off. I don't want someone around me who adopts an air of spiritual superiority and looks down his or her nose at everybody else. I don't care who you are, you haven't arrived, friend. You'd better get down off your high horse. "Pious" has a dictionary definition, which I think all of us need to understand. This is true piosity. It has to do with devotion to deity. Not "putting on airs" in front of other people, but devotion to deity, according to the dictionary.

A truly pious person has a walk with Jesus Christ that enables him to stand on his own feet, to vote his own convictions—not those of other people. A truly pious person is the kind of individual who can move into a new community and know what to do in that new situation because he knows who he is. That's true piosity.

Did you know that statistics show there are more lost people in the United States of America than in any one of the 108 nations of the world to which Southern Baptists send foreign missionaries? Did you know that you can step out of this chapel when we conclude and you will be in one of the largest unevangelized nations on the face of God's earth? Only China and the Soviet Union have more lost people than the United States.

Let's get a little closer to home. I was in a meeting on Monday with some of the folks from the Louisiana Baptist Convention offices, and Charles Harvey reported that last year, out of approximately fourteen hundred Southern Baptist churches in the state of Louisiana, 241 of them reported no baptisms last year—not one—241 churches in lovely Louisiana! How many of those churches were served by New Orleans Seminary graduates? Probably a large portion!

Pious means reverence for deity and devotion to divine worship: reverence for deity, who is God incarnate in Jesus Christ, who urged us to be obedient to his commands. He's the one who has commanded us to disciple all nations.

I read an interesting little poem the other day. It doesn't rhyme, but it's a poem. Someone wrote:

When a church seeks a pastor, they often want the strength of an eagle, the grace of a swan, the gentleness of a dove, the friendliness of a sparrow, the night hours of an owl, and when they catch that bird, they expect him to live on the food of a canary.

Let's stand and bow in prayer. "Father, grant that everything that's done on this campus, in the classrooms and in all of our activities, shall prepare the students who come this way to serve thee with efficiency and effectiveness, and may they be used of thy Spirit to bring in thy kingdom in a world like ours. In Jesus' name, Amen."

Landrum P. Leavell II has been president of New Orleans Baptist Theological Seminary since 1975. Prior to this he served as pastor of First Baptist Church, Wichita Falls, Texas, and several churches in Mississippi. A graduate of Mercer University (B.A.) and New Orleans Seminary (B.D., Th.D.), he has several books that have been printed by Broadman Press.

The Pilgrimage of Peter

CARLTON L. WINBERY

One of the people around Jesus about whom we have the most information is Simon Peter. Not only do we know much of what he did, we also know something of how he thought and felt. We can observe his spontaneous outburst as one of the inner circle of Jesus' disciples and his preaching and debating in the early church as recorded in Acts, Paul's writings, and 1 Peter. While his words are mediated to us through others (Mark, Luke, Silvanus, Paul, etc.), something of the person and his pilgrimage are clearly there with all of his human frailties, yet passionately progressing toward the character of his Lord.

Though the picture of Peter in the gospels will vary according to which gospel we read, he clearly is a first century Jew who wants a Messiah who will overcome the enemies of Israel and establish his victorious reign in Jerusalem, where his followers will share in that glory. All of that came crashing down in the catastrophic events of the crucifixion. Then came the resurrection, but even that did not end the pilgrimage nor make Peter's understanding complete. After the events in Jerusalem leading up to the ascension of Jesus the Christ, Peter's pilgrimage is most graphically revealed in Acts, read in the light of Paul's letter to the Galatians.

WHERE PETER CAME FROM

When Cephas came to Antioch, I opposed him to his face because he was worthy of being condemned. For before some of the men came from James (the Jerusalem Church), he regularly ate with Gentile Christians. But then when these man came, he withdrew and separated himself because he was afraid of the Jewish Christians. The rest of the Jewish Christians joined him in this hypocrisy, with the result that even Barnabas was enticed into their hypocrisy. But when I saw that they were not living in accord with the truth of the gospel, I said to Cephas before them all, "If you a Jew have already lived like a Gentile and not a Jew, how can you now compel the Gentiles to become Jews?"

A very important question asked among the commentaries on Galatians and Acts is when this event took place, in relation to the events recorded in Acts. The assumption is often made that it took place after the Jerusalem conference, recorded in Acts 15 and Galatians 2:1–10. This seems natural, for the event is found in Galatians after Paul's description of the conference. However, Paul nowhere indicates that he was recording the events in sequence.

There exists the possibility that in the course of talking about his relationships with the leaders in Jerusalem, he considered it necessary to explain this event that had happened with Peter in Antioch. His whole defense of the apostleship in Galatians was probably due to the claim by others who had come to Galatia that they had the backing of the great Apostles in Jerusalem ("those reputed to be pillars"—Gal. 2:9). Thus they forced him to explain his disagreement with Peter.

When it took place is not indicated by its place in the text of Galatians, only that it did happen and why. On the other hand, Luke does not necessarily record all of the events of Acts in chronological order either. The famine mentioned in Acts 11 was probably (according to the Jewish historian, Josephus) after the death of Agrippa I, recorded in Acts 12. I assume that the statement of Peter at the conference recorded in Acts 15 in his most mature statement concerning the issue of relationships between Jews and Gentiles in the church.

The beginning of Peter's pilgrimage was as a first century Jewish fisherman. He lived in Galilee near the Lake called Gennesaret (Tiberius or Galilee). There he made his living until he was bidden to follow Jesus. This he did, thinking that he was the Messiah expected to come, get rid of the Romans, and establish the rule of God in Israel.

His life was a roller-coaster ride of ups and downs, of failures, mountain top experiences, disappointments, doubts and finally resurrection, ascension, and Pentecost. Surely, at Pentecost he was on top of himself and now ready to face anything. But the church still had to make that transition from a Jewish group of followers who were convinced that Jesus from Nazareth was the Christ, the risen Lord of Israel, to those who fully understood and were willing to give all to take his message of redemption to the whole world. Peter was still not quite there. The picture of his timidity in Galatians 2:11–14 is just beneath the surface of the episode recorded in Acts 10 and 11. The fact that Luke devoted a chapter and a half to this one episode indicates that Peter, as well as the Jerusalem church, took some convincing. The experience at Joppa was described by Luke in detail. Luke stated clearly that the Holy Spirit was working in the lives of all concerned. He led Cornelius to Peter and Peter to Cornelius. As a result of the visions and the experiences of the Spirit, Peter began the sermon to Cornelius and his house with the statement, "I perceive that God is no respecter of persons" (10:34). This was Paul's point exactly in their controversy at Antioch.

THE JERUSALEM CHURCH

Peter closed the sermon to Cornelius' house with the statement, "The Prophets bear witness to the fact that every person who believes in him receives forgiveness for sins through his name" (10:43). Before he finished speaking, Peter and "the believers from among the Jews who came with him" (10:45) could behold that the Holy Spirit had fallen upon all those who heard the word. Luke emphasized the amazement of those Jewish Christians who had come to Caesarea with Peter. They were witnesses to the fact that Cornelius, a Roman Centurion, had received the Holy Spirit. Then they asked Peter to stay with them for a few days.

Later in Jerusalem some of the Jewish Christians took issue with Peter. They were intimidating as they made their charge: "You associated with uncircumcised men and you ate with them!" (11:2). Then Luke narrated how that Peter told them the whole story of how the Holy Spirit had worked to bring about the events that had transpired in Joppa and Caesarea. Peter remembered that Jesus had promised the Spirit to the disciples. Then, what is surely the punch line for Luke, was spoken by Peter: "If therefore God gave to them the same free gift [the Holy Spirit] as he did to us when we believed in Jesus the Christ as Lord, who was I to presume to stand against God" (11:17). A very similar statement was made by Peter at the conference in Jerusalem: "God who knows the heart bore witness to them by giving to them the Holy Spirit as he did to us. Thus, he made no distinction between us and them but cleansed their hearts by faith" (15:9–10). Peter's point was that for him to refuse to associate (even to eat) with them would be the equivalent of refusing God!

Contrary to the Antioch experience of timidly yielding to the pressure of the Jerusalem Christians, Peter had now in Jerusalem, in the assembly, articulated the basic "Pauline" belief that all people stand before God equal (Romans 3:22b–23). Clearly, Peter knew then that to refuse to eat (or share in any other way) with anyone in whom God, the Holy Spirit, resides is to refuse to fellowship with God. The Jerusalem congregation under the leadership of James drafted a letter to Antioch indicating acceptance of the Gentile Christians without the need of the Jewish ritual of circumcision.

OUR OWN PILGRIMAGE

The experience of many seminarians began as did mine,

in a small southern, rural town. In my home town, many men were proud of the fact that no blacks lived in our town. Some even said that no black person dared to disembark from the bus that ran through on the way between the larger cities. The lumber company owned all the houses in town. No one lived in the houses except those who worked at the mill. Only whites were employed at the mill. Only whites attended our church. The mill was later sold to a large lumber conglomerate. They built a new mill. They now hire black and white persons to work at the mill. Still only whites attend the church in the town.

The journey from then until now has not been an easy one, just like Peter's journey was not an easy one. I was voted out as pastor of one church because I timidly suggested that we were conducting church contrary to the Bible by excluding people on the basis of external appearance. Being intimidated, as was Peter, I found ways to skirt that issue for a long time in my next pastorate. As I later realized, partially under the influence of Peter's pilgrimage, I was doing them a disservice. Amazingly when I did speak out again, God had already created a loving group who themselves realized the rightness of an all inclusive policy for any church which wants to be God's instrument of redemption in the world. They supported me, encouraged me, provided a fellowship where God could nurture me to a more mature love for all people.

In recent months I have heard of some of our students and graduates who have faced similar difficulties, voted out or forced to resign. It seems impossible in this day and age that there are some Baptists still trying to be church and still locking God out of their fellowship.

Someone has said that the eleven o'clock hour is still the most segregated hour in American society. That is a tragedy. The very people who have the answer to hostilities in the world, the alienation, the bitterness, the strife, are ruling themselves out of God's solution to the problems. As Paul said of Peter, they are not living according to the truth of the gospel (Gal. 2:14).

I think that the time has come that no church which systematically excludes any people from their fellowship on the basis of color should be able to find a God-called person to be their pastor. As Will Campbell said, "But there is real doubt that it (any church) can both neglect its mission *and* deny its very nature and yet remain the church"[1].

As a church which belongs to Christ—voluntarily giving up its own freedom to be "slaves of Christ"—we deny the one who owns us by refusing fellowship with any in whom the Spirit of God dwells.

NOTES

[1]*Race and Renewal of the Church*, (Philadelphia: Westminster Press, 1962), p. 11.

Carlton L. Winbery holds degrees from LA College (B.A.) and New Orleans Baptist Theological Seminary (Th.D.), where he is Professor of New Testament and Greek. After serving as pastor of churches in Louisiana for twelve years, he taught at Baptist College at Charleston, S.C., before coming to New Orleans Seminary in 1976. He is co-author of Syntax of *New Testament Greek* with James A. Brooks, and has written several articles for Baptist journals and Sunday School literature. Having led various study/travel programs at NOBTS, he also studied for a year as visiting Professor at Regent's Park College at Oxford University (1984).

Guess Who Is In Chapel Today?

HAROLD T. BRYSON

Revelation 1:9–20

Sometime between 9:30 A.M. and 10:00 A.M. on Tuesday, Wednesday, and Thursday a familiar question circulates among faculty and students of New Orleans Baptist Theological Seminary. It is, "Who is speaking in chapel today?" In some cases the question arises either out of legitimate interest or mere curiosity. In other cases the question comes as a condition for attending chapel. Let us be honest with each other—who speaks in chapel determines if some people will attend.

Guess who is coming to chapel at New Orleans Baptist Theological Seminary this year? The lineup sounds like a Who's Who: Dr. William Pinson, Dr. Frank Pollard, Dr. Lynn May, Dr. Tal Bonham, Dr. Albert McClellan, Evangelist Eddie Lieberman, Bo Baker, and many others. These speakers represent homiletical heavy weights, outstanding orators, adept administrators, and powerful pulpiteers. You will want to hear each person. In fact you will want to make chapel a part of your week on three occasions.

About two years ago Dr. John O. Strange, professor of Hebrew and Old Testament, talked outside my office between the hours of 9:30 A.M. and 10:00 A.M. A student asked Dr. Strange a question, "Who is in chapel today?" The professor's answer impressed me. He said, "I do not know who is singing. And I do not know who is preaching. But I know the Lord will be there. Will you join me in meeting with him?" That response struck me. The Lord comes to chapel as often as his people gather to worship

101

him. It should not take homiletical heroes, peerless pulpiteers, or religious clowns to draw his people to attend worship.

Let's get the perspective of the New Testament churches. Their great affirmation was the presence of the living Lord among his people. The author of the Revelation depicted Christ "in the midst of the seven candlesticks." The author of Revelation stressed the presence of the living Lord among his people. The Revelation was written fifty or more years after the earthly life of Jesus. The writer's main emphasis was not on the speaker or pastor in the seven churches, but on the presence of the living Lord among his people. On the Lord's day the first century believers gathered to celebrate a presence not to perpetuate a memory, not to fabricate a story but to enjoy the presence of a Saviour.

What has happened to the presence of the Lord? Has the passing of the years diminished his presence? No, the Lord still comes to his people. So, guess who is going to be in chapel this year? The Lord will gather each day as his people assemble. Nothing will affect chapel attendance more than God's people celebrating the Lord's presence. Chapel attendance can be increased with famous personalities, reprimands from those in charge, and infliction of guilt. But better chapel attendance will come as a result of celebrating the presence of the living Lord among his people.

The Lord comes to chapel. He speaks by various means and through various personalities. When the Lord comes to chapel, he is busy. Using the first three chapters of the Revelation, let us examine the activities of the Lord in the midst of his people.

THE LORD ATTENDS CHAPEL TO CONFRONT US WITH THE ACTUALITY OF HIS PRESENCE

John gave a sevenfold, symbolic description of the risen Christ. 1) His head and his hair were white . . . as snow. 2) His eyes were as a flame of fire. 3) His feet were like burnished brass. 4) His voice as the sound of many waters. 5) In his hand seven stars. 6) Out of his mouth proceeded a sharp two-edged sword. 7) His countenance was as the sun. The description depicts Christ's presence on earth, seeing, moving, knowing, and judging. The risen Lord dwells *now* with his people. This Christ whom John described is actually present with us today.

The Lord made his presence known to each one of the seven churches. Look at the Lord's identification to each one of the seven churches: 2:1; 2:8; 2:12; 2:18; 3:1; 3:7; 3:14. Look at the reality of his presence. The expression in Rev. 1:13 depicts a real person present among people. Jesus is *meso*; in the midst of his people. This expression dispels the idea of a perpetuated memory, the need to beg for one to come, or the appearance of a ghost. No, Jesus actually abides in the midst of his people.

The presence of the Lord in our chapel is real. He comes, and we can experience the reality of his presence. Let us acknowledge the presence of the Lord in our chapel services. Irrespective of who sings or who preaches the Lord attends chapel. We do not create his presence. He actually comes to be with us.

The expression in Revelation 1:13 not only depicts a real presence, but it also depicts a celebrated presence. Who is in the midst of the seven candlesticks? He is the supreme Son of God. The Lord, creator and redeemer of the world, visits his people. He is a celebrity. Jesus Christ comes to be with us. Someone greater than a denominational dignitary attends our chapel. Someone greater than a peerless preacher visits. Jesus Christ, the Son of God, comes to our chapel.

When the Lord confronts us with the actuality of his presence, we make various responses. The presence of such a dignitary causes us to respond with awe. "And when I saw him, I fell at his feet as dead." John adored the living Lord. He responded in awe. Coming to chapel and confronting the living Lord causes us to get to know him. We confront the Lord and say, "I stand amazed in the presence of Jesus the Nazarene."

The presence of the living Lord causes us to respond with our best. Speaking in chapel challenges the best within us. Each speaker knows the presence of scholars and the critical eye and ear of students. Years ago Dr. A. J. Gordon said, "I do not know if I went to sleep and had a dream or fell into a trance and had a vision. But it was Sunday morning, and I was on the rostrum. The people were coming in. I noticed one visitor in our midst. The visitor, a stranger, sat by a deacon." As Gordon preached he made a mental note about the stranger. Dr. Gordon asked the deacon, "Who was that stranger? How did he get out without coming by me?" The deacon spoke, "Pastor, that was no stranger. Did you not recognize him? That was our Lord."

A. J. Gordon said he awoke from the dream with fire on his mind and his heart. He claimed the promise of the lord, "For where two or three are gathered together in my name, then am I in the midst of them" (Matthew 18:20). Dr. Gordon's preaching was revolutionized when he recognized the actuality of the Lord's presence in his services. He was made vividly aware that when God's people gathered, Jesus came to be with them.

Guess who will be in chapel this year? If you are not careful, you could miss the actuality of his presence. You could be more aware of human efforts and human leaders than the Lord. Nothing helps our chapel more than the realization of the Lord's presence.

THE LORD ATTENDS CHAPEL TO COMPLAIN ABOUT THE REALITY OF OUR ERRORS

John reported the words of the risen Lord to the churches. The Lord complimented the churches, but he also complained about errors among God's people. For two of the churches, Smyrna and Philadelphia, there is nothing but praise. For two others, Sardis and Laodicea, there is nothing but censure. For the churches in Ephesus, Pergamum, and Thyatira both praise and censure are intermingled.

The Lord complained about the errors among his people. He complained about the lost love in Ephesus, about the eroding truth in Pergamum, about the license for hedonism in Thyatira, about the false reputation of Sardis, and the lukewarmness of Laodicea. The Lord's complaints are not cruel. He simply wanted to help correct errors.

When the Lord comes to chapel, he complains about our errors. The Lord has the penetrating eyes as a flame of fire. Out of his mouth proceeds a sharp two-edged sword, capable of piercing our problems. The Lord complains not to devastate us, but he complains to help us move from where we are to where we ought to be.

Soon after I graduated from New Orleans Baptist Theological Seminary, a layperson furnished some funds for preaching professors to visit recent graduates who majored in preaching. I received a notice that one Sunday one professor would visit my worship service. He came. Several weeks later another professor came to visit our worship services. After each service, the professor evaluated. Each one had compliments, but each one had complaints. They called attention to my errors. The only way to grow is to be aware of faults.

The Lord attends chapel, and he complains about our faults. Yes, seminary students and faculty have faults. Whatever displeases the Lord in your life, he complains about it.

When the Lord complains, what should be our response? One appropriate response would be to listen and let him tell you the problem. To every one of the seven churches, the Lord said: "He that hath an ear, let him hear what the Spirit saith unto the churches." So many times we refuse to listen to the Lord's complaints.

Another appropriate response to the Lord's complaints would be to take action in correcting the fault. To many of the churches the Lord said, "Repent!" Do something about the errors. Coming to chapel offers an opportunity to change our mind. The Lord does come to chapel. He complains, but also helps us in the processing of getting rid of sin.

THE LORD ATTENDS CHAPEL TO COUNSEL US
WITH THE NECESSITY OF HIS ORDERS

The Lord wanted to help his people. He did not want just to complain. He offered advice and counsel to his people. When the Lord attends worship with his people, he helps them.

The Lord challenged the churches of Asia Minor. He counseled the church at Ephesus to return to their first love: he counseled the church at Smyrna to be faithful; he urged the church at Pergamos to fight the Nicolaitans; and the church at Thyatira to get rid of an evil woman. He urged the church at Sardis to repent. He promised the saints at Philadelphia that he would help them during the time of temptation. He counseled the church at Laodicea to get concerned about spiritual matters. The Lord counsels his church.

Guess who is coming to chapel this year? The Lord comes to church. He gives us his orders. We forget so soon his orders. The Lord comes to chapel to give us the orders for evangelizing. "Go ye therefore, and teach all nations, baptizing them in the name of the Father, and of the Son, and of the Holy Ghost. Teaching them to observe all things whatsoever I have commanded you: and, lo, I am with you alway, even unto the end of the world" (Matthew 28:19–20). The Lord gives orders to teach others to observe. There are so many implications of the gospel. The Lord gives orders to minister to the needs of human beings. The Lord gives orders to forgive others. The presence of the living Lord gives orders.

Football is one of my favorite sports. There is an amazing rhythm about football. The team runs a play, and then the team huddles. The team runs another play, and then the team huddles. Why is there a huddle? The team gets the play, and then they run it. Coming to chapel means we come to get the plays of our Lord. We go from chapel to obey his orders.

The Lord does attend chapel. We celebrate his presence. We listen and heed his complaints. We learn his orders. But there is yet another activity of the living Lord among his people.

THE LORD ATTENDS CHAPEL TO CHEER US WITH QUALITY OF HIS ENCOURAGEMENT

The risen Lord came to troubled people. The people at Smyrna fought the persecutors. The believers in Philadelphia faced trials from those of the synagogue of Satan. The Lord came in the midst of these churches and cheered them. He came with the quality of his encouragement.

The Lord comes to chapel because he knows seminary students and faculty need encouragement. He comes to cheer us. In God's work people get tired and weary. They become discouraged and get weary in well-doing. The Lord comes to chapel to cheer the weary.

In God's work people have doubts. This could be especially true as we examine scholastic matters. The Lord comes to cheer us with his great assurance.

God's people come from a competitive world They struggle to survive. With drooping spirits God's people come to worship. They encounter the risen Lord, and they go away with their spirits strengthened. Only the risen Lord can really cheer the weary.

At the age of eleven I became interested in bicycle racing. At a local car race track they had bicycle races. I competed, and I won all the races. A local bicycle shop came to town with some three-speed British bicycles. They were determined to beat me. I was apprehensive. The night of the big race came. Over twenty bicycles lined up to race. We pedaled hard. I led the race from the start. My legs were tiring. The three-speeds coming on my side intimidated me. Then on the home stretch, I heard my father standing by the fence, "Go, Harold, go!" With that encouragement I reached down for more and finished first. The risen Lord also cheers us.

Guess who is coming to chapel this year? Guess who is in chapel today? The risen Lord is with us. Have you met him? Surely the presence of the Lord has been in this place.

The Lord comes to be with us in worship. He also goes with us to help us with his service.

Harold T. Bryson was born in Tupelo, Mississippi. He graduated from Mississippi College with a B.A. degree and from New Orleans Baptist Theological Seminary with the B.D., the M.Th., and the Th.D. From 1956 to 1976 he served as pastor. In 1976 he joined the faculty of New Orleans Baptist Theological Seminary where he serves as Professor of Preaching and Chairman of the Pastoral Ministries Division. He is the author of seven books.

Go, Buy The Field

JOE H. COTHEN

Jeremiah 32

The army of the King of Babylon was then besieging Jerusalem: and Jeremiah the prophet was confined in the courtyard of the guard in the royal palace of Judah. . . This is what the Lord says: I am about to hand this city over to the king of Babylon and he will capture it. . . Jeremiah said, the word of the Lord came to me. Hanameel, the son of Shallum your uncle is going to come to you and say, buy my field at Anathoth, because as nearest relative it is your right and duty to buy it. Then, just as the Lord had said my cousin Hanameel came to me in the courtyard of the guard and said, buy my field at Anathoth in the territory of Benjamin since it is your right to redeem it and possess it, buy it for yourself. I knew that this was the word of the Lord, so I bought the field. . . This is what the Lord Almighty, the God of Israel, says, take these documents, both the sealed and unsealed copies of the deed of purchase and put them in a clay jar so they will last a long time. For this is what the Lord Almighty, the God of Israel says. Houses, fields, and vineyards will again be bought in this land (Jeremiah 32:2, 3, 6, 14).

Of all the philosophers and prophets that I have read, none surpasses the wisdom and the accuracy of Murphy. His many laws have proven to be inexorably accurate. I would share with you briefly some of his astute observa-

tions given for the hard times in your life:
1) Friends will come and go, but enemies accumulate.
2) Beauty is only skin deep. Ugly goes to the bone.
3) No one's life, liberty, or property are safe while congress is in session.
4) If you are feeling good, don't worry; you will get over it.
5) When you have climbed the ladder of success, you will then discover that it was leaning against the wrong wall.
6) If everything seems to be going well, you obviously don't understand the situation.
7) No good deed goes unpunished.

Now, Jeremiah would have said that Murphy is an optimist. Things were not going well for him or for Judah. Nebuchadnezzar's army laid siege to Jerusalem. A part of the people had already been taken into Babylon. The cordon steel was now drawn tightly about the neck of the nation. The city was in imminent danger. These were the last days for Jerusalem. After a lifetime of service, the prophet still wondered in his soul at the purposes and the timing of God.

Though he loved his nation and Jerusalem, it was his divinely appointed duty to predict its demise. His preaching was not popular. His mood was grim. His life was constantly in jeopardy, and, at this moment, his future was uncertain. So it had always been with God's preacher. At the beginning of his ministry he was confronted with an irremediable dilemma. Now, from God he heard an irreconcilable demand which prompted him to his irrepressible dependence upon God for an irrefutable deliverance.

I. IRREMEDIABLE DILEMMA

His call faced him with an irremediable dilemma. The call itself had been most unwelcome. To a country boy in Anathoth, to be called to a city ministry in Jerusalem was a frightening experience. He said, "The Word of the Lord came to me saying, . . . before I formed you in the womb I knew you, before you were born, I set you apart. I appointed you as a prophet to the nations." Jeremiah's response at that time had been, "Ah, Lord God, behold I cannot speak, for I am a child." That unwelcome call was followed frequently by undeserved discouragement. In the 15th chapter, the 10th verse of his prophecy, we hear him wail, "Woe is me, my mother, that you bore me, a man of strife and contention." Obviously the deacons' meeting had not gone well that night. He was the subject of unfair treatment. He complained, "Why does the way of the wicked prosper? Why do all that are treacherous thrive? Thou plantest them and they take root. They grow and bring forth fruit." To put it in the seminary parlance, "How come it is that the folks over at the ice house can afford doughnuts and Church's fried chicken when I have to go home and eat a bologna sandwich for lunch?" Unbelievable demands were made upon him. God said, "Jeremiah, if you think it's difficult in Anathoth, wait until you get to Jerusalem. If you have raced with men on foot and they have worn you out, how can you compete with the horses? If you stumble in safe country, how will you manage in the thickets by the Jordan?" He was subjected to unyielding pressure. So often he wanted to resign. He wanted to quit. He wanted no further part in this dreadful ministry. But then he said, "If I say I will not make mention of the Lord nor speak anymore in his name, there is in my heart, as it were, a burning fire shut up in my bones and I am weary of holding it in, and I cannot." He learned this lesson: you never back away from the call of God to be his messenger. No, not ever!

II. IRRECONCILABLE DEMANDS

God said to him at the inception of his ministry, "You will have little or no results, but preach on!" For all of his adult life Jeremiah had preached and worked faithfully. No converts, no new missions established, no new churches, no pastor search committees ever came to hear him. No salary raises, no new pastorium, no anniversary recognitions; but God said, "Preach on."

Lies and criticism befell him, but God said, "Preach on, preach on." He was used and abused by the people, but

God said, "Preach on." The king said, "Is there any word from the Lord?" Jeremiah said, "There is." But the king didn't like that word. Nevertheless God said, "Preach on." The circumstances were impossible, but God said, "Preach on Jeremiah, preach on."

Some of the people had already been taken to Babylon. Nebuchadnezzar was at the wall. The countryside had already been over run. The siege camps and battle preparations were going on outside. The attack mounds were being piled high against the walls. The battering rams moved ponderously into place. The catapults creaked into position. Devastation and horror held the people in their vice-like grip. There will be no tomorrow. But God said, "Preach on, preach on." God's commands to him were incredible, but God said, "Preach on." The Lord said, "You are going to have a visitor here in jail. Hanameel, the son of Shallum, your uncle, is going to come to see you and he is going to offer you such a deal that you can't refuse. He wants you to buy his field in Anathoth. Back up there where the countryside was already in the control of the Babylonians."

What a time for kinfolks to visit! Sure enough, Hanameel came, and he said, "I want you to buy my field in the territory of Benjamin. It is your right to buy it and to possess it for yourself."

The prophet must have wondered. Here I am on the brink of sharing the disaster of my people. That country at Anathoth was already under the heel of the oppressor. No one could go back out there any more. Was this some sort of a sick joke? But to Jeremiah's amazement God said, "Buy the field."

Jeremiah had difficulty reconciling his circumstances and his faith. Circumstance says the time is wrong; faith says today is not all there is. Circumstance says the enemy is without; faith says God is within. Circumstance says defeat is certain; faith says victory is ultimate. Circumstance says we have no future; faith says God holds your future. Circumstance says I can't afford it; faith in God says you cannot afford not to obey God. Circumstance says the situation is hopeless; faith in God says there is tomorrow.

So, "I bought the field," Jeremiah wrote. No future, no money, or no need for it. He knew he would never put a plow into its fertile soil. He knew he would never drop a seed into the furrow there. He knew that he would never wield the scythe at the harvest time. He knew he would never fill a barn with the rich fruits. He knew he would never eat bread from that field as long as he lived.

"I don't know why," said Jeremiah, "but God commanded and I bought the field. Hanameel left with a chuckle, counting his shekels. Baruch, a faithful colleague, began the job of putting the deed into a clay jar and sealing it up. Jeremiah could see there were question marks all over Baruch's face concerning the prophet's sanity, and in total frustration Jeremiah bowed his head. At such a time, under such circumstances, he had bought a field. This drove him to irrepressible dependence.

III. IRREPRESSIBLE DEPENDENCE

I think Jeremiah probably waited until it was dark. Then he realized at that moment the money was gone and the useless deed was sealed up in a jar. Baruch was asleep. When nobody could see him any longer, the weeping prophet got off in a corner alone with God and the tears of frustration flowed. He cried out, "Ah, Lord God, Ah Lord I know that you know what you are doing. I know you never make a mistake. I know you always know best, but why Lord, why? I am broke, I am discouraged, I look like a fool in the eyes of others. Why Lord, why?" Prayer was his only hope, yet it had always been his best hope.

Dear friends, you can muzzle a man so that he cannot articulate another syllable, but you can never keep him from praying. You can chain his body to a dungeon wall, but his heart will always escape through prayer.

Detrich Bonhoffer shared this experience. He wrote, "In me there is darkness, but in Thee there is light. I am lonely, but thou leavest me not. I am restless, but with Thee there is peace. In me there is bitterness, but with Thee there is patience. Thy ways are past understanding, but thou knowest the way for me."

You may isolate God's man from other men, but you can never cut him off from the resources of God. You may impoverish his existence, but you cannot deny to him the riches of God's grace. Others may turn their backs and know him not, but God will always meet in the secret place with him. The door has never been forged, the dungeon has never been built, the army has never been assembled that can keep God from the side of his own when he hears them cry, "Ah, Lord God."

Dear friends, when the Christian cries, "Ah, Lord God," it shakes the foundations of hell. It frightens the world. Satan looks in concern at what is about to happen, for when the Christian seriously cries, "Ah, Lord God," something—something is going to happen.

IV. IRREFUTABLE DELIVERANCE

This act brought for Jeremiah, and ultimately for the nation, irrefutable deliverance. Ah, the present was always there. It was a troublesome present. God said, "They have done evil in my sight from their youth, they have provoked me, they have aroused my anger, they have kindled my wrath, they have turned their backs, they would not listen, they set up their idols, they built their high places, they sacrificed their babies to Molech in the Valley of Hinnom." They did all these things, but God is not through. Churches may refuse to evangelize, but God is not through. Preachers have quit working at the task God has given them, but God is not through. No loyalty to God may be in the pew, no obligation in the heart for kingdom service, but God is not through. Cut-throat tactics among Christians may live, denominational in-fighting may be going on everywhere, but God is not through. We are having too many meetings with each other and not enough meetings with him. There is too much concern about our fringe benefits and not enough concern about the blessings we are supposed to be to the nation, but God is not through. He said to Jeremiah, "Buy the field." God is not through.

Daniel stood in that lion's den unafraid, because God is not through. Jesus stayed on the cross, he walked out of the tomb, he is coming in glory again, because God is not through. To Peter on Pentecost he said, "You stand up and preach, God is not through." Paul, write to us from your prison cell: God is not through. John, look beyond your Patmos and tell us what you see on the other side: God is not through.

"Someday, someday," God said, "I will bring them back to this place and let them live in safety. Deeds again will be written. Land again will be sold. Homes again will be built. Crops again will be planted." Call them back to God and the goodness of his ways. Call them back to prayer rather than promotion. Call them back to a love for the house of God. Call them back to compassion for the lost and dying nations. Call them back to an awesome reverence for the God who loves them. God is not through. Call them back to an eager anticipation of his coming again and our place with him. Call them back to a realization of what is important and what is not important in their lives.

While I was pastor on the Westbank, I had the privilege of serving as Chairman of the Committee on Order of Business one year for the Louisiana Baptist Convention. It was an experience to be treasured. In that capacity I had to sit down at the front. I usually was a good Baptist and sat in the back. But I had to sit on the front. Usually the afternoon sessions of some of our conventions don't have that many thrills about them. Reports and other things. On the agenda for that afternoon was a recognition of retired preachers. When the time came, the man who was to do the recognition called the name of an elderly preacher I did not know. I heard that he was 90 years old.

They called him to the platform, and a couple of men had to help him up the steps. They had a plaque and the man who was giving the plaque read it with the recipient's name, and then he placed it into the trembling hands of that old senior citizen of heaven. The old fellow stood there for a moment, looked at that plaque, and sort of shook his head.

Then, as though he was oblivious of all of us who were there, he spoke to someone we could not see. He lifted that plaque up over his head, and he said, "Mama, look what they done give me down here. I'll bring it with me when I come." Then he stopped and thought, he said, "Naw, Mama, we ain't going to need nothing like this when I get up there."

That old preacher, sometime, some place had bought a field. He had trusted God and obeyed when it looked impossible to make it. I think when Mama went to Glory, he and God had another understanding. The field down here, faithful service and obedience down here, for a home for him and Mama up there, and it would be a house not made with hands, eternal in the heavens.

Preacher, the devil may be circling your camp, but don't give up. Don't you quit. Buy the field, God is not through.

Help us to remember, our Father, as we face the circumstances of this moment that the future of all believers is in the hand of God and in that we rejoice. Help us today to be obedient, to buy the field, to serve, regardless of the problems and leave the rest up to God. In Jesus name we pray. Amen.

Joe H. Cothen has been on the faculty of New Orleans Baptist Theological Seminary since 1977. He served as Professor of Pastoral Work until he was elected Vice President for Academic Affairs in 1982. Prior to this he served as pastor of Oak Park Baptist Church in New Orleans, Louisiana, and other churches in Alabama and Mississippi. He received the B.A. degree from Mississippi College, the B.D. and Th.D. degrees from New Orleans Baptist Theological Seminary, and the M.A. degree from University of Southern Mississippi. He has authored *Equipped for Good Work*, *Come to Bethlehem* and *Preacher's Notebook on Isaiah*.

The Deliverer

CHARLES GRAHAM

Judges 13:1–5

Morning Seth. A drink of water from the cistern? Sure, help yourself. The water's down some, but lower the jar a ways and you'll reach it.

Your're right, it has been dry this fall. Looks as though we have missed the early rains. But the Lord gave us all we needed last year. The latter rains will come. The crops will make it through. Got all the water you need? Good.

Seth, I've wanted a chance to talk with you. I've seen you grow into your teen years. You have a whole-heartedness about you in your work, your games, your friendships. The other boys respect you. You seem to see clearly the things that matter most.

Have you taken the long look? Have you thought of the ways God has gifted you? Have you considered His claims upon your life? What about His high calling to enter into a personal covenant of faith with Him?

You say you know those are important matters—and they are a real challenge to you—but that you're not ready to make that kind of decision?—that you're still young and there's plenty of time?

Let me tell you about a young man I knew when I was your age. I'd heard about him since my earliest years. You've heard of him too. He lived right here on the slopes of the Sorek Valley. His name was Samson. He was a Nazarite as you probably know—a separated one. His parents were godly people.

There wasn't much to be glad about in those days either. But good news about Samson spread even before he was

117

born. The people said, "Have you heard what the Lord has revealed to Manoah and his wife? You'll believe it if you talk to them—see the expressions on their faces! Their son, Samson, is going to begin to deliver Israel out of the hand of the Philistines!"

The first time I saw him he looked like a king. The kings wear their hair long, too, you know. The head-band most of them used to wear has become a crown now for some. Samson, with his long hair circled with a purple band, looked more royal than the kings.

I was carrying a message one day for my parents to some relatives who had moved up into the hill country. Philistine strength was spreading inland from the coast even then; and on a ridge up there I met a group of their soldiers. The one in charge was a tough-looking fellow. I didn't like his face. And I liked the look of the iron weapon he was carrying even worse!

He ordered me to carry a load of their baggage. I told him I was on an errand, and due home the next day. I found out then just how little public relations with our people counted with him. He forced me to lug that load up to their camp site. Once there he made me water boy and never let me get out of sight.

Later, I heard him tell one of the others that they'd be heading home in three days. They'd take me with them and make me their "go-fer" at the home base. What's a "go-fer"? Oh, that's an old Semitic term for "errand boy." The Philistine said my folks would just have to think a lion or a bear had gotten me.

So, I became their prisoner-servant out there at Gaza. I was sweeper, scrubber, messenger and—of course—water boy. I dreamed of the day when I'd be home-free again—when I and all our people would be delivered from Philistine domination.

Under the Philistine thumb like that, I began to think more and more about Samson. Now and then I got bits of news about him from conversations I overheard. Things would get real quiet when somebody was talking about his strength. I kept saying to myself, "One day soon he's going to get on track and really start doing what the Lord intended him to do."

But a good many years had gone by already, and the weeks and months were still slipping by. All he did was to draw the Philistines into contests, play games with them, rile them and retaliate against them. God had given him such great gifts and such an opportunity. How our people needed his leadership.

When our folks went over to the coast they would walk with a soft tread near the Philistine towns. But when they cautioned Samson not to agitate the Philistines, he'd throw his head back in a booming laugh and say, "What else can you do for entertainment around here!?"

In spite of what I knew about his escapades, he continued to be my big man in the land. I'll admit I enjoyed the fact he kept the Philistines wondering where he would turn up next and what he would do.

You can be sure that they didn't give him the key to any of their cities. But after he carried off the Gaza city gates one night, I guess they figured it didn't matter one way or another!

I heard that those gates lay up in there in the hills toward Hebron for months. The Philistines never did send for them. They claimed they had a good supply of spare gates. The real reason: they didn't want to provide the perfect ending for the story our people were telling everywhere. They knew it would take at least ten men to lug the things back home.

Samson was a one-man army. Yet he never boasted about his strength. I'll have to say that he lifted the morale of our people. He restored a measure of their pride. One of their own was a winner. The haughty Philistines looked toward him with respect.

But to Samson, all life was a game and all time was a summer afternoon. He was a man of courage and action. But he bothered little to look beyond the present moment. After all, he could handle anything with his brawn. Little thought was needed, little work or planning—little, if any prayer.

When friends would ask him to go with them to the place of worship, he would say, "Aw, if I went up there, the roof would fall in!" If they persisted, he would say, "I know you're right. I'm gonna surprise you one of these days—I really am."

Somewhere deep inside he knew that his strength was from the Lord. But he came to take if for granted and to have little concern for the Lord's use of it.

Samson could subdue a lion but could not control his own appetite. He would feast on roasted grain, fish and wine at a Philistine party, then sit back with a big sigh and say, "Man, it doesn't get any better than this!" The sad thing was it never did.

As a Nazarite he was meant to be a walking protest against Canaanite paganism. But he was satisfied with the idea that he had the world in a jug and that he could rout the Philistines with a jawbone. He became the nonchalant Nazarite who went a game too far. So, one day, the news ran through the streets of Gaza: "They've captured Samson!" I know it hit all our people hard. But to a boy working for the Philistines against his will, it was like being run over by a cartload of green corn.

He'd made a fool of himself at the house of a woman right here in the Sorek Valley. He'd already broken two of the Nazarite vows: he'd handled corpses—even eating honey from inside the dried-up carcass of a lion. He had indulged in Philistine wine.

Now he had as good as despised and broken the third vow: he had allowed his uncut hair to be shaved away. The Lord had departed from him and his strength was gone. I know the Philistines must have watched him until they were sure of that. But then they laid hold on him and paraded him down to Gaza.

I'll never forget my first sight of him after that happened. I didn't know they'd put out his eyes. The renowned free spirit had become a blinded bald eagle. He stumbled into Gaza a helpless trophy of his own careless self-will as much as a prize of the Philistines. He had reveled in the gifts God had given him as though both he and the gifts would last forever. He had trusted in physical strength and that was gone. He had suddenly realized he had very little else.

They put brass shackles around his ankles and set him to work at the task that would get the biggest laugh. The man of the wide-open spaces was reduced to the tedious, monotonous task of cranking a grain mill. The Lord had set possibilities before him as wide as the horizon. I couldn't stand to watch him laboring hour after hour in that grain shed.

Along with my other jobs, they gave me the responsibility of leading him around the prison. He learned my name and often talked to me. I seemed to remind him of his own boyhood. He talked about his parents and their faith. He talked some about how he might have served the Lord and his people. But mostly he dwelt on getting even with the Philistines. His hearing was keen and he knew—even better than I did—when it was safe to talk.

Once, for a few minutes, he talked about my life. He told me to be as strong in body as possible, but admitted that other kinds of strength might be more valuable. Physical strength alone hadn't been enough for him. "Maybe," he said, "the truly strong man is strong in his faith and loyalty to the Lord."

He didn't talk like that again. But I couldn't forget those sightless eyes and that deep voice. That day, the Lord set the direction of my life.

The Philistine leaders called their celebrating people together at the temple of their god, Dagon. They gathered there to offer sacrifice and praise. They shouted, "Our god has delivered Samson into our hand!" They were claiming that their pagan god had delivered the Lord's deliverer into their hands. It was the worst time of my life.

When they had gotten happy on their wine they shouted, "Make Samson put on a show for us." I soon got orders to guide my charge out into the temple court to amuse them.

Three thousand Philistines were on the roof, crowding to the edge for a good look. A crowd, that included their rulers, watched from ground level beneath the roof. It seemed to me that our slow walk across that open court was endless. All eyes were on us. But, finally everything was set for the command performance.

However, the Philistines had made a fatal mistake. They had sent us to a spot between the pillars supporting the roof. In a whisper, Samson told me to guide his hands to those pillars. The next thing I knew, he was praying. He prayed for strength to make the Philistines pay for his two eyes. Then in a low voice he said to me, "I'm going to count to three. When I say 'three' you get out from under this thing in a hurry—no, you'd better take off on two." Well, I decided to run on *one*, and I did.

I'd taken several running steps and was in the clear when I heard stone scrape against stone. There were shouts of alarm and panic, the crashing of stone and timber, the sounds of human agony. All eyes were on the collapsing temple. Nobody even noticed my flight. I just kept running toward home 'til I was back among my own people.

The Philistines allowed Samson's family to come down and take his body for burial. Maybe they felt that mockery and vengeance had spawned enough abuse and death. They also may have felt a grudging respect for their enemy.

In a way, Samson's life closed with a victory. But the ghastly event was the violent goodbye of the man who might have been. He never fought the fiercest forces. He went to a worship place and the roof fell in. But it was the wrong roof, the wrong time, the wrong result.

He had needed to let the roof fall in on an appetite out of control—on the stubborn self-will that had taken control—on the game-playing that kept serious thought at bay—on an ungrateful and undevoted spirit. But he waited too long. When the roof fell, it fell in on Samson. So, Israel lost the deliverer it had never really had.

Seth, one day the Lord is going to send us a deliverer. One who knows where the real enemy is—who does not react to wrong simply by retaliating, but overcomes wrong with righteousness—who grows in wisdom as well as in stature, and in favor with God and man—who is doing the great work of God and cannot come down to a life of little games.

Right now, we can devote our lives to the Lord and let him show what he can do with each of us. The word of the Lord is rare in our day, because the Lord has so few who're willing to listen. But now, there's a young man up at Shiloh who says from his heart, "Speak Lord. Your servant is listening." So the good news has spread to Dan and Beersheba that the Lord has a prophet at Shiloh!

Do I really think the Lord has something to say to *you*? Seth, I believe he has been speaking to you all the while that we've been talking.

How can you respond, you ask? Let's pray together. You could confess to him your need of his strong mercy and make your vow of commitment to him. Then, I suggest we leave early in the morning for Shiloh. I believe you and the Lord's young servant up there would have many things to talk about together. And you'll begin to see how much more the Lord, our real Deliverer, has to say to you.

Charles E. Graham is Professor of Old Testament in the School of Christian Training at New Orleans Baptist Theological Seminary. He served as pastor of churches in Alabama for twenty-five years. An alumnus of Samford University (B.A.) and N.O.B.T.S. (B.D., Th.D.), he has written for the *Adult Teacher*, Caribbean Christian Publications and *Proclaim*.

The Lord Is My Shepherd

GEORGE W. HARRISON

Psalm 23

Psalm 23. The Shepherd Psalm. You may ask, "Why choose a scripture which is so well known as this? Can you say anything new about it?" Probably not. But I shall believe that it's important to say something true about it even if you can't say something new. A long time ago someone brought a message on the 23rd Psalm. If I knew who it was I would tell you. This speaker helped me to find a structure for this psalm that I have not found since, and I remembered it. This person suggested that we let one word designate—capsulize—each of these verses of the psalm. And since each one of these words starts with a "P", it made it a good bit easier to recall, to memorize, than if it had been a full sentence or if it had been something like alphabet soup!

This person suggested that as we read this psalm, think of it first of all as a *personal* word. Almost everyone quotes Psalm 23 verse 1 as the keystone of the whole psalm. It is more than one of the six units. It is the essence of the psalm. "The Lord is my shepherd; I shall not want." This verse makes a declaration that this psalm is personal. I, the sheep, have a personal relationship to the shepherd. I, the pilgrim, have a personal relationship with that guide. I, the guest, have a personal relationship with my host. It's a personal psalm. I believe 17 times the first personal pronoun—I, me, my—is found. No apologies to those who would say, "Could we not say 'our'?" The Lord's prayer is one of those "our, we, us" matters. But there is a time for what my late father-in-law used to call sanctified selfishness. You must make sure you have a shepherd. He may not

THE LORD IS MY SHEPHERD

be our shepherd, or their shepherd, but he is my shepherd.
The Lord is my shepherd, I shall not want. To me this
makes a very bold statement. Imagine one of David's hand-
ful of sheep. He may have had two handfuls of sheep, but
I don't think he had a hundred. Each one of those sheep,
whether they were two dozen or more, could look up at this
guide and say, in the language of sheep, "That's my shepherd." Not, I have one twenty-fourth interest in that guide
there. The sheep think differently. They don't divide the
corporate profits. They know that when they hurt their
shepherd helps them. When they get lost, the shepherd
finds them. When they break a limb, the shepherd carries
them in his bosom, and he is especially kind to those with
lambs. The Lord is my shepherd.

We have three children. They are all three adopted. They
all three happen to have their birthdays on the third day of
the third month, March 3. I've never heard my son David
say, "I am one of his three children," but always, "That's my
dad." My daughters likewise will say, "That's my mother."
They don't say, "I have a one-third interest in this corpora-
tion." Why? If Janet is hurting she's got Dad's ear. Or Car-
olyn or David. Sheep understand that. Human beings
sometimes are slow to learn it. If one member of my body
suffers—it may be small and insignificant—but the whole
body joins in the sob. This shepherd, Psalm 23 says, personally speaking, is my shepherd. And because he is mine,
all mine, I shall not lack.

The New International Version says "I shall not be in
want." Basically it means, I shall lack for nothing that is
needful for my growth, my health, my safety, my development. A little girl is said to have paraphrased it this way:
"The Lord is my shepherd; that's all I want." All else is
commentary. If one establishes the priority of the Lord as
my shepherd—all of me, all of him, all together—he or she
has the essence, probably, of what this psalm is saying.

The second verse, with a "P" beside it, would stand for
a *provision*. My God not only is personal, but also he is the
person who provides. Sheep know that the shepherd provides pastures that are safe and pastures that are beautifully

filled out with grass. At drinking time there is going to be a brook of gentle stillness, of quietness, and there's going to be a restoration of whatever they have in the way of fatigue, disease, fear, or whatever. He makes me lie down in green pastures and we all know when you see cattle or sheep lying down, they've been fed to the full and now are resting. He leads me beside the still waters. Not just that the waters are still, but they impart a stillness as though the sheep are speaking the language of Psalm 46, "Be still and know that I am God."

Basically this second verse talks about a provision or provisions. Sheep needed green grass, waters of quietness, and restoration. We need it. We need to be filled, soothed, and restored. The Lord is our provider. The sheep could say, "My shepherd will make adequate, yea, abundant provision," and Paul would say in Philippians 4:19 "My God shall supply all your needs." Needs, notice, not wishes, wants, or desires. "My God shall supply all your needs according to his riches in glory in Christ Jesus." So verse 2 continues the personal pilgrimage saying, "Not only do I have a one on one relationship with my shepherd. But this shepherd makes provision. Abundant provision."

The third verse leads us to the third "P" and that's *pathway*. Sheep are not known to find their way home easily. In fact, they apparently are about the most easily disoriented animal there is. I heard Billy Graham about 25 years ago at one of his stadium appearances relating the difference between a sheep and a goat. He said sheep lose their way easily. They have no built-in instinct. They nibble at one blade of grass after another until finally they're out in the wild somewhere and bleat pitifully. Their nose doesn't help them to find their way back. Their little short legs don't give them much vantage point. On the other hand, a goat is a different matter. Billy Graham told how he and his boys had one of those smelly mountain goats around in the mountains of North Carolina where he lives. And this goat continued to be a nuisance, butting people. So he and the boys put that goat in a pickup truck and took it ten miles away and turned it loose on the other side of the mountain.

Would you guess that when they got back, that goat was waiting for them? That goat had loped over the hills. You can't lose a goat. But sheep lose themselves. A pathway, as through this personal providing God makes a path. He guides me in paths of righteousness for his name's sake. There weren't many good roads in those days, but when a wagon rattled down the muddy trails it left some ruts. Some people said "don't get in a rut." Better in a rut than the ditch. And those who have tried to ride those hogback roads in Kentucky after a rainstorm are glad to settle for some comfortable ruts sometimes. It is better than not getting there. The Psalmist wrote, "My shepherd leads me in paths of righteousness"—right paths—"for his name's sake."

The fourth verse speaks of a *presence*. The language is now going to shift from "I, he" to "I, thou." Yea, even though I walk through the valley of the shadow of deepest darkness, even death, I will fear no evil for thou art with me. Thy rod and thy staff they comfort me—the presence of the Lord. We need the presence of the Lord and we need to know that he is present. We need to celebrate his presence. To affirm his presence. To remind ourselves the Lord is here. "Lo, I am with you always, even to the end of the age," are among Jesus' last words, to his assembled church. As when the Lord called Moses, saying "I will be with you." As when the Lord reassured Jeremiah, "I will be with you." When the Lord called you, you somehow became convinced of the unalterable presence of the Lord, whether in this geographical location or that vocational application. The presence of the Lord. So this personal God is personally present.

Verse 5, of course, is *preparation*. A wise shepherd prepares the pasture for his sheep. A wise host, or hostess, makes wise preparation for their guests. Parents make preparation for their children's needs, educationally and every other way. This fifth verse talks about preparation. You prepare a table before me in the presence of my enemies. Anointing my head with oil, filling my cup to the brim. A wonderful banquet, even in the midst of enemies: either glowering, wild animals or hostile, would-be assassins.

What if you were a missionary in Beruit, Lebanon, held up in some cellar or hideaway. Though I walk through the valley of deepest darkness and have no embassy flag flying over my doorstep, yet, I will fear no evil for thou art with me. That's the presence claimed by every missionary—home, foreign, or any other.

And finally, the *prospect*. The psalmist said if the Lord has been present with me, provided for me, made the pathway plain, what are our prospects? Paul would say he who has begun a good work in you will perfect it; will complete it; will finish it. But this sheep doesn't have that kind of assuring language. This ancient verse says, surely goodness and mercy shall pursue me, not just tag along behind, following meekly. Surely goodness and mercy shall pursue me all the days of my life. And as for the future, where the Lord is, I will be. Wherever the Lord is, I shall dwell, I shall abide in the house of the Lord forever.

So we see that this psalm has unfolded for us. A person; one who has provided, one who has shown us the path and the way, the truth, and the life, one who is present in all circumstances. One who is even now preparing better things for us as we prepare to serve him better.

George W. Harrison has been Professor of Old Testament and Hebrew at N.O.B.T.S. since 1960. Prior to this he taught at Georgetown College, KY., from 1955–1960. A graduate of Georgetown College (B.A.) and Southern Seminary (B.D., Ph.D.), he has written several series of lessons for the Baptist Sunday School Board. He has served numerous churches as interim pastor and Bible teacher.

God's Scrapbook

JERRY E. OSWALT

Malachi 3:13–18

The child is excited. His eyes are dancing with anticipation. This is his first big parade. Obviously both he and his father are novices because they are so unprepared for viewing the parade. They have no large bag to put their throws in. They have no customized ladder upon which to perch above the crowd.

The motorcycle policemen inch down the street, lights flashing, moving the crowds back to the curbs. The parade is about to begin! As anticipation builds, the child's heart feels like it is riding on a pogo stick in his chest. He yells for attention as the floats creep by. The riders do not look his way. He jumps, extending his arms almost out of socket and screams for a throw from the riders. One float passes, then two, three, and four. Still not a single prize is in his hands. He begins to be disillusioned.

Have you ever felt like life was a parade and all the throws were going over your head? You may have felt that way when your friend was called to a church and you weren't. Or, you may have sensed the disillusionment when your neighbor's kids didn't go berserk when they breathed the air of New Orleans but yours did. Or, how about the time your car was stripped while the one parked next to it was untouched. Maybe you felt the pain and wondered why when your wife had trouble adjusting to the radically different life of a seminary family while others seemed to make the transition without a hitch.

We all have experienced the despair created by the perception that the choicest throws of the parade of life are going to others. And it is torturous enough when the people catching those throws are good guys like us, but when they are the bad guys, the hurt is more intense. Somehow we never can fully accept the scenario of the bad guys getting the breaks while the good guys get the brokenness.

If you know what it is like to feel like life is a parade and all the throws are going to others, you can identify with post-exilic Israel. They anticipated a quick restoration of their land when they were released from Babylon to return home, but by Malachi's time (over 100 years after the return), they were still nothing more than a vassal to Persia. Jerusalem was still nothing more than a country town, and the Temple, though it had been rebuilt, could not compare to the beauty and magnificence of Solomon's Temple. They complained to God about their situation saying, "What gain is there to caring about the requirements of God? It is futile to serve him." They called the arrogant blessed of God and remarked that even those who challenge God escape.

Now some folks say those were the bad guys in Israel who were saying those things. And the good guys were the ones who are mentioned in verse sixteen. "Then those who feared the Lord talked with each other." In fact, most of the commentaries argue that. Personally, I identify with both the guys who complain and the guys who fear the Lord. I don't see why they can't be one and the same. In fact, I find the two intermingling within myself. And even though, by the grace of God, I have not turned away from him when the throws have not been coming my way, I know in my heart that I've been tempted.

William Thompson, in his book *Preaching Biblically*, cautions us as preachers, when we are interpreting the Word to others, to be very careful not to always identify with the good guys in the text, but with the bad guys as well. I think that's good advice in order to correctly interpret Scripture and make it live for people today.

But you know the feeling. You know the disillusionment. You know the doubts. And you know the temptation that such experiences bring into your own life to become a little careless about living for God. Well God had some wonderful words of comfort for Israel in verses sixteen through eighteen, which are also wonderful words of comfort for us when we sense this temptation in our lives.

"Those who feared the Lord spoke often to one another." You identify with that. You have known, when you have had your moments of disillusionment and when you have had your moments of doubt, that you still could go to your quiet place; or you, in fellowship with another believer, could speak reverently and lovingly about the great God of compassion who you know loves you and is with you, even when the throws aren't coming your way. So, the Lord makes special provisions for those who fear him, even in the midst of our doubts and disillusionment. All of the provisions are promises—some people call these "pie in the sky." I call them "bread for daily living." I need them every day. Some people refer to them as the "opiate of the people." I refer to them as the "opulent promises of a great, mighty, loving, and sovereign God."

First of all, God remembers his people. "A scroll of remembrance was written in his presence, concerning those who feared the Lord and honored his name." The Book of Life, the Book of Remembrance, the Scroll is frequently mentioned in Scripture, both in the Old Testament and in the New. More often than not, it refers to a book in which God writes the names of his people. And so Moses, in Exodus 32:32, prays, "Oh God, if you will not forgive Israel my people, then blot my name out of the Book of Life." And Paul, in Philippians 4:3, is complimenting those faithful women and others who have assisted him in the ministry when he says, "Their name is written in the Book of Life."

The mentioning of the word here has to do with a kind of record that God keeps of his people and their faithfulness to him. Many believe that the reference point for this was the Persian king's habit of keeping a record of the good deeds of his subjects who were loyal to him.

My precious mother, who went to be with the Lord in 1984, kept a scrapbook of my ministry. I didn't know that it was in existence until about a year before she died. It is difficult for me to explain to you how much it meant when she brought out that scrapbook and presented it to me. It is one of the greatest treasures I have, because she kept it in pride and in love. And you know what? She only had in it the limited achievements and successes of her son. You can look intensely through the book and you will not find one mention of failure, not one mention of a moment of laxity. Why? Because Mother didn't remember those things; she chose not to remember them; she looked them square in the eye and, because she loved me, she said, "I won't remember that anymore."

Likewise, God's scroll of remembrance, I like to think, is a kind of scrapbook of all the good things that we've done in ministry, in discipleship, and in service to one another in the name of Christ. To be sure, this Book of Remembrance is solidly founded on the grace of God. And nothing that we have done merits our names being there. But God loves us so much that he likes to keep up with all of the good things. And you won't find failures there. They've been washed away in the blood of the Lamb—past, present, and future. It's a book of remembrance of the good things only.

But also, we find encouragement here in our times of disillusionment, by seeing in verse seventeen that God keeps us. "They will be mine," says the Lord Almighty, "just as in compassion a man spares his son who serves him."

I have a friend who, a few years back when his children were young, used to frequently go through this litany with them. And I must confess, I borrowed the litany from him and used it with my children when they were younger, because it impressed me so.

He would say, "Do you know how much I love you?" And his child would say, "No, how much?" cringing with excitement, because he knew the answer. He had heard it before. And then his daddy would say, "The whole world full!" And then the father would say, "Do you know why I love you?" And then the child would say, "No, no. Why do you love me?" And then the father would say, "Because you're mine and nothing can change that!" What security that instilled in the lives of those children! How it helped them to face life with courage and healthy self-esteem! But more significantly, how it helped them to have a correct understanding of the Heavenly Father and of his love for them! God keeps us, because he loves us. We're his possession, and nothing can change that.

I saw a sermon title not long ago which has a little bad grammar in it, but I like it anyway. It simply said, "God's Grip Don't Slip." He keeps us!

Also, we find here that God will make a distinction one day between the good guys and the bad guys, between his people and those who have not chosen to be his people, between the redeemed and those who are yet lost in their sins. He will make that distinction. He will separate the sheep from the goats, the wheat from the tares. He will give all the bad guys black hats and all the good guys white hats. He will make the distinction for the whole universe to see— a distinction in terms of situation. His people will go to the glories of heaven. Those who are not his people will go to the condemnation of hell. God in his time will make that distinction.

Meanwhile, there is even greater comfort in realizing that the distinction is already being made. If we, like folks in verse sixteen, are fearing the Lord and talking with each other about him, and knowing that he listens to us and hears us, if we are intimate with the Lord and intimate with one another in Christian fellowship, therefore growing in Christ-likeness, (although we may not have reached the prize of complete Christ-likeness), then we are in the race and that is distinction. People know who we are because of our commitment to Christ, which creates the greater opportunity for his transforming grace to flood our lives and make us new people.

So you see, God is throwing us things all the time— blessings that are the superior blessings. Oh yes, we might be wishing that we had a choice trinket like a cup or spear thrown to us. But we have to be contented, we think, with the less expensive, little beads and necklaces and what-nots that come our way.

No, if we have the eyes to see, and I think we do, we can see that the throws that are the best are the intangible ones. In thinking about this, I imagined God throwing his spiritual blessings, which are the best ones, in the shape of blown kisses. And so he throws us constantly his kiss of love, his kiss of loving-kindness, and his kiss of great tolerance. He is constantly pouring upon our lives the best blessings of all. And that, more than anything else, will help you and me not to grumble and mumble when the choice trinkets of life do not come our way; but to thank God that he keeps us, that he remembers us, that he distinguishes us from the ungodly, and that he gives us great spiritual blessings always in heavenly places with Jesus Christ.

Jerry E. Oswalt has been Associate Professor of Preaching at the New Orleans Baptist Theological Seminary since 1986. Previously, he served as an administrator and faculty member at William Carey College in Hattiesburg, Mississippi. He has also served as the pastor of churches in Mississippi and Alabama. A graduate of Mississippi State University (B.A.) and New Orleans Seminary (B.D., Th.D.), he has written Sunday School lessons for *The Baptist Record* and articles for *The Theological Educator*.

When You Mess Up

Psalm 13

The title of the message today is "When You Mess Up."
Notice I did not say, "If you mess up," but "When you mess
up." From my vantage point, looking at my clay feet, I am
assuming that somewhere, sometime, when you least expect it, the candid camera of reality will catch us all in a
genuine, thoroughgoing, eighteen-carat mess up. And
when it does, what do you do?

Do you sing a happy song and pretend you didn't mess
up? Will you deny that life sometimes gets out of focus and
that "sometimes it's marked savagely by disequalibrium, incoherence, and unrelieved asymmetry," as Walter Brueggemann has put it? Perhaps it's laudatory that the church by
and large has continued to fling happy songs into the face
of the disorder, darkness, and disarray often encountered
in life, and thus the church insists that "nothing shall separate us from the love of God." I think maybe that is laudatory.

Such a mismatch of life disoriented and faith-speech that
is oriented is Habakkuk's great "nevertheless." Listen to the
prophet's speech from Chapter 3, verses 17 and 18.
"Though the fig tree does not bud, and there are no grapes
on the vines, though the olive crop fails, and the fields
produce no food, though there are no sheep in the pen and
no cattle in the stalls, nevertheless I will rejoice in the Lord.
I will be joyous in God, the God of my salvation."

But singing happy songs may not be evangelical defiance
guided by faith. Instead, it may be frightened: the denial
and deception that does not want to acknowledge or expe-

rience the disorientation of life. Such a denial and cover up seems odd to me, odd especially for passionate Bible users, since there are so many biblical songs of lament—protest and complaint about the incoherence of life. To go on singing happy songs in the face of raw reality is doing something very different from what the Bible itself does.

When sickness struck, enemies arose, and tragedy erupted, the Israelites protested, lamented, mourned, and complained. Such songs question reality for a person who has pretended that life is well-ordered, when in fact it is not. The denial may include a lost job, a broken relationship, a medical diagnosis, or some other tragedy. At such a time to sing a sad song may seem to the world to be an act of unfaith and failure. But for the trusting community, it should appear as bold faith. It is bold in its insistence that such disorder is a proper subject for discourse with God. Such songs say that God is present in, participating in, and attentive to the darkness and the weakness and the disorder in life. He is a God of sorrows and acquainted with grief. Mystery of mysteries, these songs often affirm that in our journey passage through such dark and deathly places, new life is given of God.

Real life has anguished seasons of hurt, alienation, suffering, and death. These evoke rage, resentment, anger, self-pity, and hatred. Is there room in your religion to express these emotions? Or, must we go on saying in the church, "We must not question God." Or, in a certain setting I have said, "I wish I had a layman to say an appropriate word," when I felt like not saying it myself.

What do you do when you mess up? When life is out of focus, when everything is not coming up roses, when you're greeted and asked, "How are you doing?" You answer, "Fine." And inside you are dying. Shall you go on lying to yourself, and especially to God? Have we thought that we might topple God from his throne if we approach him with words of accusation? Lord, how long? Will you forget me forever? How long will you turn your face away from me? How long must I wrestle with these thoughts and I cannot find answers? What do you do? Well, I have three words for you and I probably have time to say all three of them.

TELL GOD HOW BAD IT IS

Tell him! In Psalm 13 something is terribly wrong in the poet's life. Something is terribly wrong between him and God. And note, if you will, he addresses God directly. "How long, O Lord?" Nothing is out of bounds. Everything is included in this conversation of the heart. To withhold part of life from conversation with God is to withhold part of life from the sovereignty of God.

The speech begins abruptly, with no explanation. While God is addressed under the covenant title Yahweh, the address is exceedingly terse. The pain is so acute, there's no time for convention or nicety. The speech is not reasoned. It's a barrage of someone in such sore condition that the accusation must be stated in its most vigorous form. And the writer does that.

What he says to Yahweh is scandalous. But Yahweh is addressed because he is the Lord of the human situation and he is a covenant partner. The poet's problem is not clear. His distress seems unending. His trouble is in part his foes. He appears near death. He may be desperately sick, but his primary concern is an apparent separation from God.

Four questions addressed to God are rhetorical in nature. They do not expect an answer. They simply voice the extreme perplexity and distress of life for the psalmist. They describe a radical disorientation. They fix the blame squarely on God. The trouble is absence of God! "Where are you, God?" Has he forgotten? Has he hidden his face? This explains the mess the psalmist is in.

It's interesting that the psalm does not state clearly what is the particular problem. I think that's fortunate. Right now, you could plug in your problem. Whatever it is that puts life out of focus for you, right now can be plugged right in. It may be a student whose wife came recently to the campus and to the city seeking employment, for the sake of bringing the family on down to join the student. While here the teenage daughter at home attempted suicide. Did God forget? Did he turn his face? Did they sing a happy song? It may be a student and his wife who have waited nine months for the birth of their first baby; their hopes are dashed to the ground when the baby is stillborn. It may be a student whose wife walks in and says, "I'm leaving you." It may be a student whose son falls off a hay truck and is killed. It may be a professor whose health fails suddenly and the future is overcast with swirling clouds of doubt and uncertainty. And it could be Judy in Hotel Dieu right now with a forty percent survival hope from chemotherapy and some other procedures related to her cancer. Judy has a ten year old daughter and a husband who waits. It could be Dr. Claude Howe's wife, Joyce, in north Mississippi who has held the hand of her mother and watched her die. It could be any one of us.

So what do you do? Do you pretend that everything is under control? Do you deny the fact? Do you repress your feelings? The psalm says, "Set your pain, your sorrow, your anger, your fear to speech. Address it to God. Tell him how bad it is." That's what Job did. Robert Frost dealing with that issue, has Job and his wife in heaven, and she continues talking about the boils—Job's illness. How different Job, who pursues his question to God for an answer. Job says, "Why, God? Why, God?" And he cries out again and again. Listen to the speech Frost puts in his mouth:

I'd give more for one least beforehand reason
    Than all the justifying ex-post-facto
Excuses trumped up by you for theologists.

Come, after all these years—to satisfy me.
    I'm curious. And I'm a grown-up man:
I'm not a child for you to put me off
    And tantalize me with another "Oh because."
Why did you hurt me so? I am reduced
    To asking flatly for a reason—outright.

I don't think he's very far from Scripture with that. Joachim

Begrich's hypothesis about the value of this kind of speech addressed to God is that grievance addressed to an authorized partner frees us—sets us free. This insight lies behind Freud's theory of talk therapy—we do not move beyond repressed memory unless we speak it out loud to one with authority who hears us. This psalm suggests that this is true not only in a counseling session, one on one, but in a worship setting when we gather together as the children of God.

ASK GOD FOR HELP

In an imperative mode—"Look at the mess I'm in," is the way Billy K. Smith would render that first phrase in verse 3. "Look at the mess I'm in." And then he says, "Answer me." "Cause my eyes to be lightened." These are commands. I think he means, "Change my situation. Give me an oracle of hope at least." You see, illness and sorrow and suffering endured long term may dim the eye. So he says, "Lighten my eye with returning health and a better oriented life." And I think the speaker assumes some rights against the throne as he does that.

The mess up is beyond the poet's fixing. Unless the Lord acts, there is no way out for him. He knows that. Look at the intimacy of the address to "the Lord, my God." This is not some pagan talking to God. This is his own child. This is a covenant partner talking to God. And that makes it different.

On the basis of that relationship he appeals to God, and then he gives God some motives for his action, in case God needs a little directing, I suppose. "Lest I sleep the death," he says. And sleep often is associated with death. "Lest my enemy say, 'I prevailed over him.' Lest my foes rejoice because I am shaken," which probably is a reference to death.

What the poet does is to make his problem God's problem. If the Lord is a partner and he's ridiculed, that is, the Lord's partner is ridiculed, then the Lord is diminished himself. The speaker tells God what he needs to know so that he can act. And then he waits on God to act. It's a long wait, a wait in the darkness of death, a wait in disorientation, a wait, as Brueggemann puts it, "until hell freezes over." It must be a long wait, for there's no other court of appeal.

Between verse 4 and 5 something happened. I don't know how long the wait. I don't know what changed things. I don't know whether he got well or whether God answered him and gave him a hope oracle or what. I don't know, but I know this. When the poet speaks again, he is headed in a new direction. What do you do when you mess up?

CELEBRATE GOD'S RESPONSE

When you've told him how bad it is and when you ask him for his help, then wait, and celebration time will come.

Three words—trust God's unfailing love. A literal rendering of that part of the verse—"I, in your *chesed*, in your covenant loyalty, have put my hope." It's a completed action verb that anchors the poet's life there securely. No matter the turbulence, the disorientation.

And then rejoice in the Lord's acts of deliverance, the Lord's freedom may be what he means.

And sing to the Lord because he has dealt bountifully. I do not fully understand the rejoicing and the singing—whether it is that these are by way of anticipation, or whether it is that an answer has come and now he does indeed celebrate. He's anticipating at least, and all of it is dependent upon his anchoring his life in God. God is a covenant partner faithful to the covenant. So what do you do when you mess up?

Well, you tell God how bad it is. You ask God for his help. and you celebrate when God responds. Now our poet sang a sad song properly. My appeal: Give the church a sad song to sing and say, "It's all right to question God. It's all right to walk right up to God. You're a covenant partner with him. Tell him how bad it is. It's all right to do that." I told Judy yesterday at Hotel Dieu, "It's all right to feel what you have felt. It's all right to say what you wanted to say. Go on to appeal for God's help, trusting in his faithful love, and when you do, rejoicing and singing will come."

"Father, I pray that we'll not be ashamed to sing a sad song and that we will put our trust and our hope in you. In Jesus' name. Amen."

Billy K. Smith is professor of Old Testament and Hebrew at the New Orleans Baptist Theological Seminary, where he has taught for thirteen years. He served as pastor of churches in Louisiana, Mississippi, and Texas for twenty-two years before coming to the seminary. He holds the B.D. (1956) and the Th.D. (1963) degrees from the New Orleans seminary. His published works include *Never Alone, Words Speak,* and volume 13 in the *Layman's Bible Book Commentary.*

Gateway Seminary Librar